Everyone's Talking About
The Power of Horses

"The Power of Horses *is loaded with heart and soul. . .and truth!
Lives [of these artists] are much richer because of their great love
and respect for horses. The amazing and colorful details unfold in
these pages.*"

> Carol Grace Anderson, M.A., author of *Get Fired Up Without
> Burning Out* and *Some Angels Have Four Paws: Life Lessons
> From Our Dogs*

"*Real country people know that you can tell the quality of a person
by the way he or she treats animals. In* The Power of Horses, *country music insider Lisa Wysocky treats a group of horses and their
famous owners in a fresh, appealing, and gentle way, revealing
insights into each artist by showing the often mystical bond each
has, or had, with a special horse. Country music fans and animal
lovers of all ages will find* The Power of Horses *both fascinating and
uplifting.*"

> John Wooley, *Tulsa World* country-music writer and author of
> *Awash in the Blood* and *Dark Within*

"*Lisa Wysocky has gathered a unique collection of stories from country music stars. As they relate their love and respect for horses, these
stars give us rare insight to the real person behind the star image.*
The Power of Horses *is truly a must-read!*"

> Loudilla, Loretta, and Kay Johnson, (IFCO) the International
> Fan Club Organization

"The Power of Horses *is a labor of love—full of heart—combining
Lisa Wysocky's love of horses with a career as Nashville's publicist
to the stars. Lisa has written a book that all horse and country music
fans will enjoy over and over.*"

> J.D. Haas, J.D. Haas Entertainment

D0905115

Sharon –
Thanks for hooking
me up with John
& Tommy. They both
had fabulous stories.
Lisa

The
Power
of Horses

Lisa Wysocky

Fura Books
Minneapolis • Nashville

Published by
Fura Books, Inc.
P.O. Box 90751
Nashville, TN 37209-0751
www.powerofhorses.com

FURA BOOKS, and the portrayal of the block letter B
with a lower case italicized f are trademarks of Fura Books, Inc.

Book design by White Horse Enterprises, Inc.

Author photos by Farris L. Poole/Studio 10, Nashville
Make-up by Cindy Kubica/Studio 10, Nashville
Western tack courtesy of Jeff Friederich
Wardrobe by Goodwill

First edition published June 2002

The Library of Congress Cataloging-in-Publication Data Applied For

Wysocky, Lisa, 1957 –
The Power of Horses: True Stories from Country Music Stars/
Lisa Wysocky.—1st ed.
p.   cm.
ISBN 1-890224-10-3
1. Country Music 2. Horses I. Title
2002

Printed in the United States of America

1 3 5 7 9 10 8 6 4 2

Although the author and publisher have made every effort to ensure the accuracy and completeness of information contained in this book, we assume no responsibility for errors, inaccuracies, omissions, or any inconsistency herein. Any slights of people, places, or organizations are unintentional.

For information regarding special discounts for bulk purchases, please contact us at
info@powerofhorses.com

Dedication

To my mother, Pat Wysocky, for always being there, and;

*to Colby for understanding that sometimes things
are more urgent, but never more important, and;*

to Snoqualmie, who enriched my life forever.

Acknowledgements

Many thanks to Keith Bartz for teaching me to keep my head up, my heels down, and my fanny in the saddle; to Paul and Julie Overstreet for many things, but especially for letting me borrow the Isuzu; Doyle and Judy Petty, for the meals and everything else through the early years; Eddie Rhines, for more than he will ever know; Mike and Wanda Webb, for their generosity; and to Bruce and Julie Diehl, for their unending support. To Mary Isenman, Edyth Burnett and all the CFSers, you've been there when I've needed you; Jolene Mercer, Cheryl Brickey, Brenda Cline, Joan Purvis, and Sandy Wilcher, thank you all for your unconditional love. My sincere appreciation to Cathy Gurley who reminded me that 'no' is just not an acceptable answer; and to Drs. Thomas Limbird and Louise Mawn, who each in their own way stitched me back together so I could finish this book.

Special thanks to Claire Gerus, without whom the idea for *The Power of Horses* would never have been generated; and most importantly thanks to the good Lord above who makes all things possible.

To our sponsors: IFCO (www.ifco.org), Rhodes River Ranch (www.rhodesriverranch.com), The HomeShow (www.thehomeshows.com), MultiMedia-Interactive (www.multi-mediainteractive.com), thank you. Please go to their web sites and learn more about these wonderful businesses. To Lee Allen and everyone at Fura Books, thank you for believing in me and in this book.

To all the artists who gave of their time, thoughts and memories, thank you so very, very much. To the many publicists, managers, tour managers and record labels, my heartfelt thanks for your unending efforts to facilitate interviews, photos, and corrections. If I got it wrong, the fault is entirely mine. Knowing that I will forget some who helped, here is a partial list, in no particular order. To those who I inadvertently left out, my apologies and my thanks. You know who you are. Thanks go to Gary Voorhis, Bill Todd, Kelly Kiral, Carol Grace Anderson, Paula Szeigis, Lisa Boullt, Susan Collier, Thurman Mullins, Devon O'Day, Joni Werthan, Julie Bush, Darlene Bieber, Tinker Eaves, Mark and Jill Sissel, Robyn Daniel, John Wooley, Ken Woods, Craig Campbell, Allen Brown, Leslie Paulin, Adrian Michaels, Holly Gleason, Amy Leintz, Chris Marcy, Sharon Eaves, Joanne Ritchey, T.K. Kimbrell, the Johnson Sisters (Loudilla, Loretta, and Kay), Joanne Ritchey, Debra Keith, Summer Harman, Lisa Sutton, Keith Bilbrey, Tricia Cramer, J.D. Haas, Kim Staciak, Nancy Henderson, Reggie Mac, Nancy Jones, Chris Hollo, Sherrie Hensley, Kyle Frederick, David Kiswiney, Terri Jo Stampley, Evelyn Shriver, Sherry Hoheimer, Woody Woodruff, Cynthia Grimson, Ron Modra, and M.B. Roberts, who deserves extra credit.

Snoqualmie, age 28, and Colby, age 4.

Table of Contents

Author's Note

I was a horse crazy kid from the time I was two until. . .well, now. The summer I turned twelve, I got a white Appaloosa mare. I named her Snoqualmie, after an area in Washington State where Nez Perce Indians once bred Appaloosa horses. Snoqualmie was my best friend.

I lived in Minnesota and during the summers of my early teen years, friends and I would play polo, or cowboys and Indians. We'd take our horses down to the lake and use them as diving boards. Long trail rides through meandering woods were a regular occurrence. In the winter, I'd hook Snoqualmie to a toboggan and she'd pull me down snow-covered gravel farm roads.

As I grew older, Snoqualmie became my 4-H project, my youth horse at local saddle club shows, and then my game horse. When I was saddle club queen, Snoqualmie was my grand entry horse. She loved pole weaving and she loved to jump. Her smooth gaits ensured that we were tough competition on a state level in Egg and Spoon.

Snoqualmie had a colt, Ben, who was as tall and lean as she was short and fat. When I was in high school, weather permitting, I'd clamber aboard while Snoqualmie was grazing in the pasture and lie backwards, facing her tail, as I struggled with homework.

When I took a job as a trail guide at a local dude ranch, Snoqualmie became my guide horse and when I began giving riding lessons, my lesson horse. I took Snoqualmie to college with me, then to a training job in Ohio and then to Washington State. She became my pony horse when I was exercising yearlings, the horse I rode to check fences, the one I chose to ride when I just wanted to ride.

When I started my own stable, she was my main lesson horse and she was amazing. When a young child was riding, she'd walk so slowly and carefully you'd have thought she was walking on egg-shells. When the rider became more secure, she refused to do any-thing unless she was asked firmly and correctly. An advanced rider could excel on her in anything from barrel racing to Dressage. When I took a terrible fall that damaged my knee and ultimately ended my training career, she was the horse I first got back up on. She was the horse that delivered me from the fear of falling again.

Snoqualmie was very intelligent and had a wonderful sense of humor. Another trainer and I once watched as she let herself out of a locked box stall, opened stall doors of four other horses, then went back into her own stall. She slammed the sliding door shut with her nose before she turned to watch all the fun. Knots and latches were no challenge and she could open the best of them.

Snoqualmie followed me South, and in her later years became my son's horse. When he was five, they'd canter together across the pasture, bareback, no bridle, her mane flying and he laughing with glee. They'd play pirates with our big black dog, Dexter, Snoqualmie alternately playing the parts of racehorse, Indian fort, ship, or flying saucer and wearing the costumes that went along with the role.

When she was in her late twenties Snoqualmie developed a thyroid deficiency, then foundered in a rear leg. In her thirtieth year, she was felled by a stroke. Snoqualmie died just before Christmas in 1992 and is buried on a farm outside of Nashville. It has become a tradition for my son and for me to visit her each Thanksgiving Day.

For twenty-three years Snoqualmie was my friend, my companion, my sister. I knew when I called her that she wasn't going to come until she dipped her head once and tilted her nose to the right. She knew during a riding lesson if I took two steps back and crossed my arms, I was going to ask the student to trot. From her I learned the important things: friendship, determination, trust and responsibility.

Since her passing I have been searching for a way to let people know how much she, and other horses, have meant to me. Through my work as a publicist in the country music industry, I realized that many stars of country music had similar experiences with a horse in their life. Maybe it was a horse they'd had when they were a child, or maybe it was a horse that passed briefly through their life more recently. But someway, somehow, either the horse or the experience left a lasting impression.

So this is my way of thanking Snoqualmie for sharing her life with me. To the fans of county music, and to horse lovers, may you have as exceptional experiences with horses as these artists and I have had. And to the horses themselves, thank you for allowing humans into your lives. We may be dumb, but we love you with all our hearts.

LISA WYSOCKY • *Nashville, Tennessee* • *May 2002*

Clay Walker

"Clay Walker must be doing something right. Since 1993 he's racked up eleven number-one singles as well as four platinum and two gold albums. It may be time to start giving the Beaumont, Texas crooner his fair dues."

Larry Wayne Clark, *Music Row Magazine*

Four platinum albums, two gold albums, and eleven number-one singles certainly categorize Clay Walker as one of contemporary country's most successful artists. Walker grew up in a musical family, and began playing guitar at age nine. By the time he was a teen, he was already playing the honky-tonks. When he was sixteen, Clay got his first taste of radio airplay when he took a song he had written to a local radio station. "I drove to the station at 2 a.m. and handed the DJ my tape," said Clay. "Unfortunately, it wasn't formatted to fit their equipment. I was heart-broken, but what I didn't realize is that they were just trying to blow me off," he laughs. But Clay didn't give up, coming back a week later with the tape properly formatted. "They took it, but told me they might never play it, and I was crushed. But as I was driving away, they played it. I couldn't believe it! I had to pull my truck over."

After building a following in Texas, Louisiana, Oklahoma and New Mexico, Clay signed to Giant Records in 1993, and released his debut album that year. Since then, not only has he sold more than eight million albums, but for five straight years Billboard *included one of his songs on its year-end top-ten country list, a record unmatched in the same period by any other artist. Additionally, for the past several years, Clay has been acknowledged as one of country's top-ten box office touring acts.*

Since 1995, Clay Walker has been the grand finale performer at the prestigious Houston Livestock Show and Rodeo. Performers earlier in the week have included Willie Nelson, Merle Haggard, the Judds, Latin heartthrob Enrique Iglesias, and Motown's Smokey Robinson—certainly an elite set of performers.

Clay's greatest loves are his wife Lori, and their two daughters, MaClay and Skylor. Clay's relationship with them and others close to him was transformed in 1996 when he was diagnosed with multiple sclerosis. Though the disease is in remission, symptoms do recur on occasion. Through it all, Clay has realized how important family and friends truly are, and is grateful to a little gray filly who helped introduce him to Lori.

"I think that the most important thing for me in life is to learn from whatever I'm doing," said Clay. "I don't really like to participate in things that I'm not learning something from and getting something out of. With horses, you learn constantly and you get so much back."

Clay began his love affair with horses at a very early age. Horses have since developed into a true passion, and the depth of his passion is very evident in his voice.

"My first horse was a Tennessee Walker named Star," he recalled. "She was a real bright sorrel with a star in the middle of her head. I was three when I got her and I remember that I named her. I had her from then until I was about six."

When he was growing up, Clay, who is the oldest of five, lived in Southeast Texas on the outskirts of town.

"We were in the middle of a rice field in the woods about five miles outside the city limits, and it was a great experience because we literally had hundreds of thousands of acres around us to grow up on. No highways or roads, we just rode horses. We had chickens, pigs, cows, and sheep, we had everything including our own garden. It was definitely a hillbilly way to grow up but I tell you, I loved it."

Eventually Clay became interested in Quarter Horses, but he was not bitten by the horse show bug until he met his future wife.

"Actually, the way that Lori and I met was through a horse," he said. "I had bought a little filly, a little gray filly. This filly's mother was a mare named Jackie Mac, and she was an own daughter of Boston Mac, who was one of the top stallions in the breed."

Clay had heard of Lori and had seen her around. He liked what he saw and had been trying to wrangle an introduction to her for months. Finally they were introduced.

"She and I started talking, and we just naturally were talking about horses," said Clay. "I told her I'd just gotten this filly that I bought about four or five months ago."

Lori asked Clay how the filly was bred. Clay explained that his filly was a granddaughter of Boston Mac, but he was totally unprepared for the conversation that followed.

"I said she was out of this mare called Jackie Mac and whoever the stud was, and Lori goes, 'Are you kidding me!' I said, 'No,' and all of a sudden I got this funny feeling because I knew the father of this filly was wasn't a big time stud."

So Clay paused for a second to try to figure out why Lori had asked if he was kidding.

"Then she goes, 'I owned that mare. I just sold that mare.'"

Based on that conversation and the mutual interest in the mare and filly, Clay and Lori were soon an item. Soon after, Clay moved the gray filly over to Lori's place.

"Every evening at five o'clock when she got off work, we would go out to the barn and work with the horses. That was our entire past-time early in our relationship. It was nothing but horses," he said.

Lori began buying older yearlings or young two-year-olds and Clay started them under saddle. As soon as the young horse was going along nicely, Lori would turn around and sell it.

"That was a nice little side income for us and it really worked out good for us in a lot of ways," said Clay. "I've started a lot of colts out and that's probably what I've enjoyed more than anything about horses, except maybe foaling. I don't do it anymore because it can be a little dangerous, but I loved starting colts."

Lori and Clay ended up naming the gray filly Takamani Tess, and after a time, sold her.

"I've thought several times of tying to buy that mare back," said Clay, "but they'd ask an arm and a leg for her now. She's a good horse, so I know they would. They wanted to use her for western pleasure, but the way she was made, she really wasn't made to be a pleasure horse, I didn't think. She had a big old hip and hind leg, and a huge gaskin. I mean she looked like a bulldog from the back end."

Clay added that he enjoys studying equine conformation—the actual build of a horse.

"I am a big fan of a strong hip with a big carry down, and a nice croup," he said enthusiastically. "That's what I've always been a fan of, because I like halter horses [horses prized for their conformation]. When Lori and I stared this, we both wanted to raise babies that would do something and would have some pretty to them, too."

At one time, Clay and Lori had twenty-five to thirty brood mares. They've since culled their herd to the top fifteen or so mares.

"I think the greatest experience that I've ever had with horses, I mean the absolute greatest is during foaling time, during foaling season in the spring," he said. "When the babies are born on the ranch, it is absolute joy. The anticipation builds—you've waited for a year for this baby—and you feel like you've picked the right stud and you've got the right mare."

Clay and Lori breed Quarter Horses and are looking for specific attributes in build, the goal being to produce world championship halter horses.

"We're looking for conformation for halter horses and in doing that, it is a science. I used to think man, this stuff is a bunch of hocus pocus," laughed Clay. "You just take two good horses and see what happens. I am now absolutely, I mean one hundred percent, convinced that it is a science. There is just no question as to who the mother and father are most of the time. You can look at the head on one, the hip and hind leg, the eye, the color, I mean you just look at them and can't believe the resemblance."

For Clay, there is nothing like the experience of being present when a new foal is born.

"There's a lot of times where the mare is having a little trouble and you're there helping them. We just had a little buckskin filly born and there's never been a buckskin born on the ranch. We've had lineback duns and red duns and just about anything you can think of, but we've had over one hundred babies and never a buckskin so this was really special."

Clay just happened to be at the barn when the mare went into labor, and he called Lori to come join him.

"We watched it together," he said, "and the little filly got up and a couple of hours later we started talking to her and petting her and imprinting her, and that is such a special time. There's just nothing else like it."

Clay says that horses have helped him many ways in life. From sharing family experiences to learning how to read people, horses have been there every step of the way.

"Lori and I have two little girls, and it has been just a phenomenal experience to be able to take your family and have activities based around horses because it is such a good, family thing," he said. "Fortunately everyone in our whole family are real animal lovers. We go to a lot of horse shows together. It's the little things that you do together that count and I wouldn't trade those experiences for anything.

"I've come to respect horse people greatly," Clay continued. "You can learn a lot about people by being around them and their horses. You can learn if that person is aggressive, if they are mean, if they are sweet. You can learn a lot about their personality by the way they treat their animals and by the way their animals act. You know, if their animal puts their mouth all over you or tries to bite you, you know that horse has no sense of discipline and that carries over to the person who cares for that horse, and what kind of a person they are. So you know what's been going on there and can figure it out in about two minutes. You can literally go into somebody's barn and let them pull their horse out, and just by the way they get it out you know what kind of a person they are."

From Star to Jackie Mac to Takamani Tess, and to all the horses in-between, and after, Clay says he can't express how deeply horses have enriched his life.

"There are so many facets where horses can fit into people's lives," he said, momentarily silenced with the thought. "Horses can be a great addition for just about anyone. You just have to find the right facet for you. A horse can be one of your best friends, or they can be a help to you in your work, or they can be something pretty just to look at. There's tremendous therapy in just looking at a horse eat. I've gotten a lot out of just sitting and watching them graze. It's amazing. If you look at it, you can intermingle horses with any part of your life. You can use horses for sports, for pleasure riding, for art forms, and to me riding western pleasure and that type of competition is an art."

But it is the special bond between human and horse that Clay values most.

"A lot of times there is a special intelligence that can only be communicated between you and that horse. Someone else may not have that connection with that same animal. I can't really explain it," he said, trying anyway. "It's love, it's chemistry, it's that deep soul recognition that you have something in common. All I know is if it hadn't been for horses, and maybe even for that gray filly, I may not have met my wife or have the family I have today."

www.claywalker.com

Clay Walker Fan Club
P.O. Box 8125
Gallatin, TN 37066

Clay at a celebrity cutting competition in December, 2001.

Chris LeDoux

"It's not how much buck there is in the horse that makes him so good. It's the spirit they're born with. You'll not find this spirit any stronger in any man than Chris LeDoux."
Bob Tallman, *Gold Buckle Dreams*

When it comes to cowboy songs, western music and country hits, Chris LeDoux is the real deal. Chris is a former world champion professional rodeo cowboy who, during his rodeo days, happened to play guitar in his spare time. He wrote songs about life on the circuit, and his music captured the romance, the freedom, the hurt and the dirt of rodeo. His music soon found its way into the hearts of rodeo fans across the country, all of whom demanded tapes of his songs. And so, Chris LeDoux recorded twenty-two albums on his own—albums filled with music about the cowboy lifestyle he lived and loved—before he landed a recording contract with Capitol Records.

Chris started playing the guitar and writing songs when he was about fourteen. Most often, his tunes reflected his love for rodeo. While still in high school in Cheyenne, Wyoming, Chris won the state's bareback title. After graduation he won a rodeo scholarship and received a national rodeo title. Chris made his first independent recordings in Sheridan, Wyoming, and over the next few years recorded fifteen albums in Nashville for his own American Cowboy label. In those days, Chris regarded the music as just a sideline to being a cowboy. But he took the music seriously enough to sell four million dollars worth of cassettes, most of them manufactured by his parents in their own home tape duplicating room, and sold out of the back of his truck.

By 1976, Chris was becoming known as a singer-songwriter of note, and his rodeo career was riding high. Chris won the Professional Rodeo Cowboys Association world championship in bareback bronc riding that year at age twenty-eight, and also picked up awards for his artistic bronze sculptures, one of a bull rider and another of a bronc rider. Chris continued to rodeo until 1984, when accumulated injuries forced him to hang up his spurs. His recording career bolted out of the chute when a mention from Garth Brooks, who sang about listening to a worn-out tape of Chris LeDoux in his 1989 hit Much Too Young (To Feel This Damn Old), *was enough to kick up national interest in this singing cowboy.*

When Chris was still in his teens, a rank bucking mare named Necklace gave Chris a motivation to succeed that he still draws from today.

As long as Chris LeDoux can remember, he wanted to be a cowboy. Some of his earliest memories are of sitting in front of a small black and white television and watching his heroes, Roy Rogers, and the Lone Ranger, and all the others who rode across our screens during television's golden era. The only difference between Chris and the rest of us is that Chris lived his dream.

Chris's first real life experience with horses, an obviously essential part of his dream of the cowboy life, took place during the summers he spent in Michigan on his grandfather's farm.

"He didn't have any horses on the place at that time," recalled Chris. "He'd had teams before, you know to work the fields with before I was born. But he didn't have any at the time I was out there visiting."

But Chris fondly recalls an old horse in the neighbor's pasture.

"It was probably about thirty years old, sway backed, shaggy hair

CHRIS LEDOUX / 11

on him and I thought he was beautiful. I can still remember walking by there and thinking, 'Man, that's a beautiful horse.'"

A youthful Chris spent hours idolizing the old horse, dreaming of the adventures they'd have when he was a real cowboy. After years of wishing, Chris finally got a horse of his own. He was twelve, or maybe thirteen.

"We'd moved to Austin, Texas and my Grandpa actually bought him for me," said Chris. "It cost two hundred fifty dollars and back in the mid-sixties that was quite a lot of money, you know, coming from a dairy farmer, so that was quite a gift."

Chris's prized present was a buckskin quarter horse that he named Comanche.

"He wasn't anything real pretty, but I thought he was another beautiful horse. He was pretty good, though. Someone had broke him and done some roping on him and as years went by I realized this guy was a professional rodeo cowboy. And finally after I grew up and started rodeoing I saw this guy around, so this horse actually came from someone who knew what he was doing, which helped me a lot in the early years, to ride a horse that was well-trained.

"I started roping on Comanche a little bit and the horse was good. He had some spirit. I'd fall off of him every now and again, But I'd run barrels and poles and rope on him, and just learned quite a bit by just living with him."

And Chris literally lived with his horse.

"We had camp outs," he recalled. "We'd ride a couple of miles alongside a crick somewhere there outside of Austin and I'd take some old dry beans with me and the dog and the horse and stay the night, cook those beans. I didn't realize that it was going to take eight hours to get them soft enough to eat! I about starved. And there was a roping arena that I'd go to. It was about three miles from our house. It seemed like it was twice a week that I'd go, and I'd tie my bedroll on my saddle and ride to this little arena and rope two or three calves. I remember it was fifty-cents a head, and then when I was done I'd go throw my bedroll under some live oak trees out there by the arena and just bed down and in the morning just get up and ride home.

"It was pretty intimate, just me and the horse and the dog. My folks had pretty much turned me loose by then. I was free. And looking back on it now, I don't think I could have been that way with my kids. That'd be pretty tough to just let a kid go ahead and do stuff like that, but they were pretty understanding and realized that I needed some room."

Shortly after Comanche's arrival, Chris realized he was destined for the life of a rodeo cowboy.

"All the kids in the neighborhood were entering youth rodeos, and I'd got in the steer riding and won a little buckle. And that was it. It was like, 'Okay, here we go,'" he said. "There was just something about rodeo and horses and livestock and that lifestyle that drew me a lot more than football, which I had also thought some about. But I wouldn't have been big enough for football anyway. Rodeo was it for me. I'd grown up watching the cowboy movies, and my heroes really have always been cowboys. To get the opportunity to be one, well, there just wasn't anything better."

Chris spent his teen years writing songs, and preparing himself both mentally and physically for the day he would be a full-time rodeo cowboy. Along the way, he heard of a rank, bay bucking mare called Necklace. She proved to be his motivation and inspiration for close to a decade.

"When I was in high school, I'd get the rodeo sports news and I'd see the horses and the cowboys and there was a horse called Necklace that was kind of the rank horse on the circuit," said Chris. "I can remember any time I'd be out training, running or lifting weights in high school, I'd think, 'Necklace, Necklace,' and it'd make me run a little faster, run a little harder, lift weights a little heavier, practice more on bales of hay, and work to get a little stronger."

At the Calgary Stampede in 1974, some seven or eight years after Chris left high school, Chris finally had the opportunity to ride this mare who had been so instrumental in putting him at the top of his chosen field. By this time, Necklace had been voted Bareback Horse of the Year four times. For Chris, it was the culmination of years of hopes and dreams, a proving ground, a validation, of years and years of hard work.

"When I first heard about Necklace, I didn't realize that I would ever have the chance to get on her," said Chris, still a little amazed that the opportunity arose. "There were other horses that were ranker than she was, later on, but she was my motivation for so long, that this one go was. . .well it was just everything to me."

Chris had her on the short go. And for him, it was a perfect scenario.

"She was back in a pen by herself and as the crowd started coming in for the rodeo you could see her start pacing a little bit. She knew what was going on. And as the band started playing, she began pacing a little more, she was getting nervous. I was back there watching her and finally they put her in the chute. She was kind of rearing up in there, and with her they said if she starts rearing up you know she's going to buck. She's ready. So I got on her and I don't think they could have thrown me off with a stick of dynamite. It felt so good. After all those years of thinking about her. . .she was great. She just fit. She just fit my style. I won the short go-round and it just felt wonderful. It was a pretty neat experience."

Chris went on two years later to become the world champion bareback rider, hanging up his spurs and chaps for the last time in 1984.

"I loved every minute of it," he said of the rodeo life. "The people, the thrill, all of it. I loved the gypsy lifestyle, just being out in nature, seeing the sun come up in California and seeing it go down in Texas, sleeping along the highway in Montana when the sweet clover is in bloom. Just living, like living on the trail, like a trail drive. We had a Chevy suburban and that was our covered wagon, our chuck wagon. I just loved the whole thing, the camaraderie, the friends you made, just being young, and wild, and free. I wouldn't have traded one of those experiences for anything."

Given his feelings, it isn't at all surprising that Chris would trade one gypsy life for another, trade the Chevy suburban for a band and a bus. But as much as he loved the rodeo, Chris said he would not advise anyone to try it before they had carefully weighed all the options in their mind.

"If you go into rodeo, there is the distinct probability that you will experience some physical pain, and the real possibility of really getting hurt badly, so before you start you need to weigh things out on a scale in your mind. On one side, you've got the fact that you can get killed, or you can get maimed for life, and on the other side you've got how bad you want it. If one outweighs the other, then you'd better go with that decision. So if you want it bad enough and if it outweighs your fear of getting maimed for life or getting hurt, then go for it. But if your reason takes over, takes the heavy end, then maybe you'd better be a doctor or a lawyer. That's really advice I'd give anyone if they were going to make any important decision. You have to realize that you might fail, but you might win tremendously, too, and in ways that you never expected."

Chris and his wife, Peggy, have five children. All but the youngest have bypassed rodeo for other endeavors.

"You know, we went through all the kids, and none of them really showed an interest in it, in rodeo, until the last one, Beau," said Chris with a chuckle. "I had a bucking machine and everything right there at the house. And finally I just gave all that stuff away. Then about a year later, Beau said, 'Hey Dad, I might wanta try to ride.' So we had to get another bucking machine."

Chris said it makes him feel really good to see his son out there.

"It's scary, too, but I can see his determination, and I think he's got the ability. He's got a lot of drive, so it's not as scary for me as when he first started out. When he first started he was hanging up a lot, getting dragged and they'd step on him a lot. But he'd get back on, get on another one. So he's got a lot of guts."

Sounds like Beau is a lot like his Dad.

www.chrisledoux.com

Chris LeDoux International Fan Club
P.O. Box 253
Sumner, IA 50674

Susan Ashton

"After doing six Christian albums in six years, making herself a household name in the Christian music industry, Ashton finally agreed with the dozens of people in her life urging her to go country."
Brad Schmitt, *The Tennessean*

When people hear Grammy award winning artist Susan Ashton sing, they find a way to work with her. Artists Garth Brooks and Patty Loveless are among the many who have asked Susan to sing on their records. Over the years, Susan has recorded six albums, sold more than one million records, and contributed to the Grammy-winning Amazing Grace: A Country Salute to Gospel *(duet with Billy Dean on* In The Garden*) and* To Come Together: A Salute to the Beatles.

When Garth first heard Susan sing, he was so impressed that he asked her to open for him during his 1994 European tour. "He was Garth, but I had never seen his concerts. I never saw the television specials," said Susan. "When I got the opening spot on his tour, I got a videotape of his concert at Texas Stadium and freaked out. I thought, 'This is what I'm opening for?!' I started having nightmares. I'd never met Garth, so I would dream that when we met he wouldn't talk to me and would make me clean the green room or something." Instead, the tour was a very positive experience for Susan and was the beginning of a strong friendship.

A native of Houston, Texas, a very shy and impatient Susan grew up listening to the legendary voices of Tammy Wynette, Willie Nelson, Waylon Jennings and Jessi Colter, as well as pop and rock acts such as Karen Carpenter, Journey, Bad Company and Pure Prairie League. Blessed with a beautiful voice herself, Susan had her first album on the Christian label, Sparrow, at age twenty and sold hundreds of thousands of albums in just a few weeks. When it came time to perform for a live audience, Susan sang at a small church in Hendersonville, Tennessee. "I had the songs from my album and no idea what to say," she remembered. "So, you know those Laffy Taffy candies? They come individually wrapped with jokes on the wrapper. I took some Laffy Taffy jokes and tried to make a story out of those. It was all I had, and it was horrible."

Horrible, but not discouraging. Susan ignored her wobbly knees and quaking body each time she stepped onto a stage. With a lot of hard work and determination, she was soon offered a country deal with Capitol Records.

Susan has said that the love one mare had for her when she was a young girl gave her the incredible confidence she has in herself today and the patience she has for others. An avid hunter/jumper enthusiast, Susan competed on the South Texas horse show circuit until her recording career took flight.

It takes a lot of confidence to admit a personality flaw to a total stranger. But then, Susan Ashton is a very confident woman. We met in the conference room of her management company, located on Nashville's historic Music Row. Unlike many of the other artists I interviewed for this book, I had not met Susan before. I had been told only that she had loved horses as long as she could remember, and that she had showed hunters and jumpers during her teens, before she embarked on her singing career. So I was totally unprepared for the bouncy, energetic, enthusiasm oozing from this down to earth lady.

Pretty and petite, Susan is very open about the fact that when she was a child, she had a horrible temper.

"Not that I would throw temper tantrums," she clarified, taking a sip of the Starbucks coffee she loves. "I just had a very short fuse. I was very impatient. I was a perfectionist. If I asked for something once, I didn't want to have to ask again. It needed to be done right then."

Susan is still a perfectionist, but the love one mare gave her dramatically lengthened her notoriously short fuse, and gave her the patience she needs today to deal with the many demands of a recording career.

Susan was your typical horse crazy kid, watching rerun after rerun of *National Velvet* and later, *International Velvet*. She covered the walls of her room with horse posters, read every book in the library that had anything to do with horses, and dreamed of riding on the United States Equestrian Team. Whenever the opportunity arose to actually go see a real live horse, Susan pleaded with her parents to take her. She even remembers repeatedly waking up her parents in the middle of the night crying desolately because she wanted a horse so badly.

When she was eleven, Susan's dream came true in the form of a six-year-old, unregistered, dapple gray Quarter Horse mare named Silver Ghost. The horse was a Christmas gift from her parents and Susan was understandably ecstatic.

"Her nickname was BeGe and she was just gorgeous," said Susan. "She had dark legs, a beautiful dapple pattern in her coat, and black and cream striped hooves. The color on her face kind of faded into a big blaze. She was just wonderful. She had all the qualities I had ever wanted in a horse. I love the feeling of having the kind of horse under you where you are never quite sure what that horse is going to do. Not that you want them to be frantic. But BeGe was very alert, and still young enough to be feisty. She was very spirited and I loved that in her."

But BeGe also had a very affectionate, loving, nurturing quality that Susan responded to as well.

"We just bonded so completely," she said. "I remember that this horse was so patient with me as a young eleven-year-old impatient girl. And she was so young herself at the time, just six. The connection we had was very unique."

Susan kept her horse across the street from her school, and every day after class she would head over to the barn to ride, or just sit in the pasture and do her homework in the South Texas sun while BeGe grazed in circles around her.

"If any of the other horses came near me to smell me, including a black Appaloosa gelding named Joe who was her special horse friend, she'd run them off. She didn't want anything to do with them when I was there. She and I were very close and she was very protective of me," Susan said. "The relationship I had with her was the ideal relationship that kids who are horse crazy dream about. I could call her when she was out in the pasture and she'd come running to me from wherever she was. She was so awesome. It just couldn't have been any better."

After Susan and BeGe had been together for about a year, there came a day when Susan's impatience got the best of her.

"I've never told anyone this story before, because this is not one of my prouder moments," Susan admitted with a deep breath and a rueful smile. "I was riding BeGe near the barn and I was asking her to do something. I don't even remember what it was, but she just planted her feet very firmly and would not do it. Whatever I was asking her to do I am sure was not a big deal. Looking back, she very probably had a good reason for not doing whatever it was. Horses are wise that way and she was not a horse with an obstinate or unwilling temperament. But at twelve, I was not seeing the whole big picture and she was, and she was kind of giving me a fit about it. Her feet were planted and she just was not going anywhere. So I screamed and yelled and kicked and yanked the reins, and when all of that didn't change anything, I jumped off and continued it all from the ground. I wasn't beating her or anything, but I was really giving her what for."

Susan and BeGe were both worked up, covered in sweat and the adrenaline was pumping. Then for some reason in the midst of all the screaming and yelling and yanking, Susan looked up saw raw fear in the mare's eyes. The fear in itself was an awakening for the young girl.

"At that point I just started bawling because I never, ever wanted an animal to be afraid of me. I loved BeGe so much. She was my best friend. But I was a kid and impatient and I didn't know how to handle things."

Tears streaming down her face, Susan took a deep breath, wrapped her arms tightly around the mare's sleek gray neck and buried her face in the warmth of her body. Within seconds, they both began to relax.

"Then BeGe put her head down over my shoulder and pressed the side of her face into me, like she was hugging me. And when she raised her head up there was dampness running down from her eyes, like she was crying, too," said Susan, her eyes welling and her voice catching at the memory. "BeGe always had this thing where she put her head in my chest and nuzzled me. And I turned to her and she did that then. She was so kind and tender to me when I had been so awful to her. But it was like she was saying, 'It's okay. I understand.'"

That moment changed Susan's life.

"It was instantaneous. Just like that," she said, snapping her fingers loudly. "It was a life lesson I will never, ever forget. I determined right then that nothing, absolutely nothing, is worse than losing your temper. Nothing gets accomplished, you alienate the people around you, you're stressed, everyone around you is stressed. I mean, why?"

The answer for Susan lay in her youth and in her heady ambitions. She wanted things so intensely that she had a very narrow focus. If, for example, she wanted BeGe to walk over a bridge, Susan didn't take into consideration that the bridge might be slippery or that the sun was in the mare's eyes and she couldn't see well, or that the bridge might be structurally unsound. Susan just focused on the specific, immediate goal and when it wasn't accomplished to her satisfaction or in her time frame, she became impatient and things would get out of hand. BeGe changed it all.

When she was fifteen, Susan started training hunter/jumpers. She bought a Thoroughbred off the racetrack and began working with a trainer named Linda Russell.

"Linda always used to tell me that I had the patience of Job, and I always used to think, 'If she only knew,'" Susan said, laughing.

Susan was quite successful showing hunter/jumpers throughout her teens. But music kept calling and the rest of us are infinitely more fortunate that she finally chose to share the extraordinary gift of her voice.

Susan says she still dreams about BeGe.

"I just really learned from her that if something is pushing you to the point of exasperation, take a deep breath and step back. Count to ten and look at the whole big picture," she said. "As I've gone through life, when things don't go the way I want or expect them to, I still have to confront people. But because of BeGe, I do it differently now. Every time I get in a situation like that, I step back, and I think of BeGe and of that day. It was a very hard lesson for me to learn but it totally changed my life for the better."

www.capitolnashville.com

Susan Ashton Fan Club
1111 17th Ave. S.
Nashville, TN 37212

Susan, age 12, with BeGe.

Bellamy Brothers

"David and Howard Bellamy, the 'International Goodwill Ambassadors of Country Music,' are highly acclaimed artists who have been known to exceed the borders of country music by incorporating strong elements of rock, reggae, and rap. They are internationally recognized as both country and pop musicians, and are among America's most successful touring artists."
USO

Howard and David Bellamy's father was an avid country music fan, and would often wake them to the sounds of Merle Haggard or Buck Owens. The brothers grew up surrounded by country music, and the harmonies and rhythms of Jamaican fruit harvesters working in the family's central Florida orange groves. Exposure to Elvis, Ricky Nelson, Buddy Holly and the Everly Brothers, as well as the British invasion and the Cultural Revolution of the sixties, resulted in the highly individualistic style and sound the Bellamy Brothers have taken on the road for more than thirty years.

The Bellamy Brother's first gig was playing for free with their father at the Rattlesnake Roundup in San Antonio, Florida. Today, their annual Snake, Rattle & Roll benefit concert takes place in conjunction with the San Antonio Rattlesnake Festival and attracts more than 20,000 people.

Howard and David played a lot of clubs early in their careers, singing backup for such R&B artists as Eddie Floyd, Percy Sledge, and Little Anthony and the Imperials. In the late sixties, the Bellamys moved to Atlanta and extensively toured the Southeast.

Their first break came with the hit Spiders and Snakes, *written by David. Jim Stafford cut the song, which went on to sell three million copies worldwide. With* Spiders and Snakes *a major pop hit, the brothers moved to Los Angeles and Howard became Stafford's road manager.*

The Bellamy Brothers then cut Let Your Love Flow, *the monster pop hit that forever fixed them in the public eye and laid the foundation of their career. The hit meant tour dates with Loggins and Messina, the Doobie Brothers and the Beach Boys. At the end of the seventies, the Bellamy Brothers hit the country charts with* If I Said You Had a Beautiful Body, Would You Hold it Against Me *(penned by David on a dinner napkin). It became their first of more than a dozen number one country singles, including* Redneck Girl *and* Reggae Cowboy.

By maintaining the same sense of fun they started with, and remaining true to their musical course, the brothers have received more nominations for Duo of the Year by the Country Music Association and the Academy of Country Music than any pair in history. And, although the Bellamys are strong across North America, they are also well established as international artists in Europe, Scandinavia and Australia. The Bellamy Brothers have always been accepted as a pop act overseas.

Between tour dates, Howard and David Bellamy return to a ranch that has been in their family since just after the Civil War. And, just as soon as he gets home, Howard Bellamy heads for the barn.

David and Howard Bellamy grew up on a working ranch in Florida. Howard is the horseman of the two, and as we chatted over a meal at a local restaurant, I learned a lot about Florida history, and about Howard's love for a very special horse.

"I guess the first experience I had with a horse was with a breed of horse we Floridians call Crackers," said Howard. "Native

Floridians are known as Crackers and some people think that's slander, but to real Crackers it's a compliment to be called one. There are very, very few of them and it was a term taken on early on in Florida."

Florida woods are thick, explained Howard, so thick that dogs and horses were often used to find roaming cattle.

"The term back then was cattle hunting or cow hunting," he said, "because to find a cow or a calf you literally had to hunt them to pen them. So cow hunters was the term used early on for cowboys in Florida.

"There is a Cracker horse that the Spaniards brought over," continued Howard. "They were probably some of the first horses on American soil. They are not a domestic animal. They were brought here and the State of Florida has preserved this breed. It is a small horse and has a peculiar gait that it walks with."

Howard added that Crackers were great for Florida because the woods were so thick that you wouldn't be able to get through with a big, wide Quarter Horse—you couldn't get into the tight places where the cattle hid.

[Due to their small size, Cracker horses became a necessary part of Florida's cattle industry, which began about five hundred years ago and thrives still today. Cowboys in Florida were called "crackers," after the sound of their whips cracking in the air. The name was also given to the agile horses so essential for working the cattle. The Florida Cracker horse descended from Spanish stock brought to the Americas in the 1500s. Continual horse trading between Florida and Cuba meant regular infusion of Spanish genes into the Florida horse population. Eventually, due to its geographical isolation, the Cracker became a distinct breed. Today, the Florida Cracker is a valuable part of Florida's heritage, though the horse is still quite rare with roughly three hundred horses having been registered. Florida Cracker horses stand 13.0-15.2 hands and weigh 650-900 pounds. Gaits include the flatfoot walk, running walk, trot and ambling or Paso-type gait.]

When Howard was quite small, the Bellamy family owned a horse that was part Cracker and, ironically, was named Cracker.

"David was not born yet [Howard is four-and-a-half years older than David] and I used to ride Cracker with my dad behind the saddle," said Howard. "This horse would jump the Palmetto patches and everything else, I mean it was a wild ride. When you got on you'd just hang on for dear life. I just remember being back there behind my dad and hanging on to the leather straps. I did get spilled a few times."

The week David was born, Howard had no preparation that he was going to have a brother.

"They just sent me off to my aunt's house that night and she woke me up the next morning and told me I had a little bother," he said with a smile. "Well I didn't know what to think of any of it. So I came home and saw David and my first statement was, 'Well, he's not gonna ride my Cracker.' I guess it was an early lesson in sharing."

The Bellamy family horses, like everything on the ranch, had to earn their keep. They didn't have a tractor so the horses had to be able to both plow and work cattle.

"You'd end up with a real all around horse, one you could take to the creek and dive off of," said Howard. "We literally used horses for everything. I remember Charlie, who was a big, red, renegade chestnut that my grandfather owned. He was a great plow horse but he ran away with three or four members of the family before they realized how bad he was.

"Then we had Tony as I got older. Tony was part Percheron and could pull a double blade turning plow and never miss a step, that's exactly how powerful this horse was," recalled Howard. "And he had the best temperament in the world. He's the one we'd actually put five or six kids on and take him to the creek and use him for a diving board. You could literally pick a newborn calf up and put him on Tony's saddle. You could put anything on his back and he never minded."

The ranch David and Howard grew up on was founded well over a hundred years ago by the brother's great-grandfather. Abraham Milton Bellamy served in the Confederate Army as a member of Chickamauga and Carolina Infantry. He was wounded at the Battle of Chickamauga and later captured in Atlanta. He was paroled from Camp Douglas, Illinois in 1865.

After the war, Abraham and his wife, Susanna, moved to Florida and settled near Darby, just north of Tampa. Today the 150-acre homestead is still a working ranch, owned and operated by the Bellamy family. The livestock consists of Brangus, Angus, and crossbred cattle; and Quarter Horses. A large variety of citrus fruits grow there as well, including oranges, kumquats, and grapefruit. Three generations of Bellamys currently live on the ranch. They also lease a nearby 2500-acre ranch, which is a calf-cow operation, and own a feedlot in Texas.

Throughout his lifetime, Howard has been around hundreds of horses, but his all-time favorite is a horse he currently owns.

His name is Cariucca," said Howard softly. "He's twenty-three now and I've had him since he was six."

Cariucca is a registered Quarter Horse stallion and appeals so to Howard because, as with the horses of his youth, Cariucca is a very versatile and even-tempered horse.

"He's a lot of horse, but still a horse you can just do anything with," said Howard. "Of course with a stud horse, and as you get older, temperament becomes a very important thing. He is by far the best temperamented cutting horse I've ever known. I rode him on a cattle drive, and they didn't allow stud horses for obvious reasons. He's the only one they ever allowed because his disposition is that well known. I took him along and he was a perfect gentleman even though he was tempted a few times, or teased I should say."

As with Florida and the Bellamys, Cariucca has an interesting history all his own.

"When I was in high school I didn't need but very few credits to graduate so I worked half a day on a huge ranch owned by the Bartell family," explained Howard. "They have a great reputation and every year now, I look forward to riding by their pasture and seeing all their new foals. Well Joe Bartell owned the sire of Cariucca. His name was Chic Black and he was a really deep bay with the black around the eyes and all the trim, really one of my favorite colors for horses. And over the years I owned three or four foals by Chic Black, so I knew what good horses they were. Joe Bartell started Cariucca, and then sold him to a Venezuelan and the horse went to South America. Then the Venezuelan married my neighbor's daughter, and they brought him back to work cattle here."

Howard remembers the first time he saw Cariucca.

"Oh, I just fell in love with him," he said. "I offered to buy him, and of course he didn't want to sell. About eight months or a year later I remember being on tour in Europe and it was like three-thirty or four o'clock in the morning and I'd just gotten to sleep. My phone rings and it's my mother and I said something like, 'Mother, this better be good.' I was so tired, but she said, 'Howard the horse is for sale.' I knew automatically which horse it was and I've had him ever since."

Howard says Cariucca is a beautiful horse and that beauty was one of the things that initially attracted him.

"But beauty is only skin deep. I've found that looking for a good temperament in a horse is such an important thing. I've made the mistake because of a beautiful color or a beautiful horse to just fall for them," he said ruefully. "With Cariucca, you could do anything. You could bulldog off him, you could rope off him, you could shoot a shotgun off him. I have had handicapped children on him, he was so well trained. His versatility has always amazed me. I've enjoyed a lot of horses, but he's been with me a long, long time and he is my favorite horse."

Age is beginning to catch up with Cariucca so Howard no longer cuts or ropes off him.

"He's very active at twenty-three, he's very fit. But he's semi-retired and pleasure riding is all we do on him," said Howard. "I just turned a young two-year-old gelding in with him in the same pasture. From the first day there was never a problem. Now they've become major buddies, inseparable. So he has a friend in this Paint colt, Ranger."

Over the years, Howard and Cariucca have spent thousands of hours together and Howard says he wouldn't trade that time, those experiences and memories, for anything.

"He's one of those rare individuals who has become a true friend," said Howard. "He is just so willing. People who knew him when he was very young said his tendencies were always that way even when he was a foal. I don't think you can really create that. It's like a person. You either are or you aren't. And Cariucca is. He is just everything I could ever imagine wanting in a horse. They just don't make them any better than that."

www.bellamybrothers.com

Bellamy Brothers Fan Club
P.O. Box 801
San Antonio, FL 33576

Howard Bellamy and Cariucca.

Ricky Lynn Gregg

"Male country music stars with big cowboy hats had better circle the wagons. There's a renegade part-Cherokee country rocker by the name of Ricky Lynn Gregg on the loose and he's burning up stages from Augusta to Anaheim."
Tom Dodge, *Heartland USA*

Rockin' country blues artist Ricky Lynn Gregg, has electrified audiences nationwide with his high-energy performances and music videos. His swarm of fans regularly travel thousands of miles to see the man perform and Ricky often repays the compliment, staying past dawn to sign hundreds of autographs.

In his teens, Ricky played in a band with two of his older brothers. Positions in a series of Dallas-based bands, including The Ricky Lynn Project and Savvy, led Ricky to a successful stint as the lead singer in the critically acclaimed rock band, Head East.

As time passed, Ricky felt a growing desire to return to his musical roots. After signing a deal with country-based Liberty Records, Ricky was named Billboard's *number-four Top New Artist for his debut.* Ricky Lynn Gregg, *the album, also made a top-ten debut on* Billboard Heatseekers. *The singles released from the album (including* If I Had a Cheatin' Heart, Three Nickels and a Dime, *and* Can You Feel It) *were among the 1990s biggest dance club successes.*

Ricky has been a finalist for Performance *magazine's Best New Country Act, including the Marlboro Music Tour. And, extra security was hired in Chattanooga, Tennessee when 18,000 fans danced in the streets to RLG music.*

Ricky is a consummate musician, having played guitar on major label albums such as Hank Williams, Jr.'s Hog Wild. *And Ricky's commitment to excellence is extended from the studio into his live show. You'll search far and wide to find a performer who puts more energy into a performance. He pours his heart and soul into each ballad, easily bending the notes with his distinctive voice. But audiences around the world come alive with the rockin', stompin' edgy country that Ricky Lynn Gregg is best known for. Ricky and his audience do have fun together.*

Ricky Lynn Gregg has covered the entire spectrum of the musical world. But in spite of his many life experiences, or maybe because of them, he attributes one of the biggest lessons he ever learned in life to an old pony named Shep.

Ricky and his four older brothers were raised on the outskirts of a small East Texas town. They spent countless hours on the seat of a tractor while learning the country values taught by their parents and the Bible. It was a comfortable childhood, filled with family and friends.

"My next oldest brother was ten years older than me," said Ricky, "so by the time I was six or so, they were in their late teens and early twenties—quite big enough to whomp on a pesky little brother."

Two of Ricky's brothers were heavily into anything that had to do with horses and the Gregg brothers soon became well known in the area for their fine Quarter Horses. Ricky's brother, Dennis, still trains horses and competes in team roping.

By the time Ricky was about ten, Dennis felt it was time Ricky had his own horse.

"I'd been riding a lot of the horses Dennis had around the place but there wasn't any one horse I could bond with," Ricky said. "At that point riding was fun, but I know now that there is a whole lot more to it when you can actually establish a relationship with a particular horse, and learn to know that horse as well as he knows you."

Dennis looked around and found an old paint pony by the name of Shep. Shep was of stock-type build with the rough coat and scaly hooves of a West Texas range horse. In fact, Shep looked as if he could have spent the majority of his life in the western part of the state, looking at cacti, armadillos and long-horned Brahma bulls. The Gregg brothers were always buying and selling and trading horses, and Ricky said he is pretty sure that the old pony was most likely traded for something there on the ranch. Ricky doesn't recall that they ever had any kind of registration papers on Shep.

"He was just a good old ranch pony who was probably ready to retire," he said.

The first day Ricky rode Shep was a day that shaped many of the fledgling singer's actions even to this day.

"In one sense, Shep, just by having been around the bush a few more times than I had, was a good teacher," Ricky recalls. "But you'll see that Shep and I didn't click. He was old, he was cranky, and he didn't have the patience for a rambunctious young kid like me. He really made me want to really learn to ride the right way because I just could not make him do what I wanted him to do. It was very frustrating. At ten and as the spoiled youngest child I felt I owned the world. And I did. Until I met Shep.

"On down the road I learned that the look Shep had in his eye the day I first met him meant that a horse was up to something," said Ricky. "Shep was a smart horse, much smarter than a farm kid like me. But at this time, I didn't recognize the look. I just wanted to get on and ride."

Ricky's brothers didn't say anything to him ahead of time; they just presented Shep to him one sunny summer Sunday as a surprise. The ranch pony came outfitted in typical Western working gear—thick, well-worn saddle pad, a heavy old saddle with wide stirrups and no padding on the seat. The bridle was well worn, and well cared for—standard for the Gregg brothers working ranch style of riding.

Ricky remembers being very excited about riding this new pony. Riding being the key word here. Ricky wanted the action more than the animal. He says he was so excited that for a few minutes he couldn't think of anything else except getting on Shep and galloping off into the sunset, just like the Lone Ranger. In a young boy's eagerness, Ricky overlooked the beginnings of a sweat on the horse's rough-coated chest. Ricky didn't catch the glare in the pony's keen eye, or the impatient flick of a long, brown tail as he excitedly ran up to his new friend. Ricky aptly describes himself at that moment as 'having more enthusiasm than sense.'

Ricky was so excited to ride Shep for the first time, that he just clambered aboard and took off across the Gregg brother's weather-beaten riding ring, just like he had imagined a thousand times that he'd do. In his mind, Ricky was John Wayne. He was an Indian flying across the prairie. He was a bank robber chasing a train. But about twenty yards out, reality and imagination came to a parting of the ways. The saddle slipped sideways and Ricky landed hard, flat on his back, in a lumpy, rocky patch of East Texas dirt. It took Ricky's brothers a long time to round up the gleeful Shep and just about as long for young Ricky to regain his breath. Ricky says the ribbing his brothers gave him hurt far worse than the fall.

"I remember lying there, wind knocked flat out of me, wondering if I'd start to breathe again before I died. My mouth was full of dust and grit and dirt and my back hurt so much I couldn't roll over to spit it all out. On top of all that, the overlying thought in my mind was all this agony was my own fault. I brought this on myself because I didn't check," said Ricky. "I didn't check the saddle to see if the cinch was tight, or to see if the bridle was adjusted properly. I knew better, but I was so excited, I just got on and took off."

Ricky says he was very disappointed in himself that day. One of the first things he learned about riding was to check your own cinch, your own equipment.

"If your equipment fails you," he says, "you have only yourself to blame."

Ricky let his eagerness for a new situation override common sense, and that's something he doesn't often do. Anymore.

It turns out that Shep was one of those wily old ponies who held his breath when being saddled. Being a new horse on the Gregg place, Ricky's brothers didn't notice Shep was holding his breath, or maybe they thought Ricky would tighten the cinch before mounting.

Or maybe they knew, and in the exuberance of young manhood thought it would be a hoot to see their kid brother dumped in the dirt. In any case, the saddle was loose and Ricky was on the road to learning a lesson he never would forget.

"I hate to say this, but I didn't have a clue as to what Shep was doing," said Ricky. "I don't know if I was slow and hardheaded, or just very young and eager. I'd like to think the latter, but it took a long, long time for me to realize that this was what some horses did. Horses learn to hold their breath when being saddled for several reasons. Either they once had someone who cinched them too tightly on a regular basis, or they are very smart. Or both.

"For whatever reason, Shep held his breath when he was being saddled. And I eventually learned never to get on any horse without checking the cinch. In fact, that first ride with Shep taught me always to check all of the important things in life yourself," said Ricky. "Check everything. If you're going for a drive, don't take someone's word for it that the gas tank is full. Look at the gauge. See for yourself. If you are the driver of the car, it's your responsibility to see that the vehicle is properly fueled. Don't just head out blindly down the road on someone else's say so. Just like when you are riding a horse, it is your responsibility to make sure the equipment fits properly and that everything is in good working condition."

Ricky took Shep's teachings with him when, as a teenager, he embarked on a musical career. The fact that Ricky was personally double-checking everything from tour logistics to technical aspects of the sound system led him to a greater understanding of his chosen profession. Today, he attributes the old pony to much of his success. Ricky is still very hands-on when it comes to his career and even though he has managers and consultants advising him, Ricky is directly involved in most of the day-to-day decisions involving his career.

"When it comes to my career," he said, "I have some very good people working with me and advising me. But the ultimate decisions are mine. It's my responsibility to know what everyone is doing for me. It's my responsibility to learn as much as I can about the business of the music business."

With business in mind, Ricky has recently taken music business classes at a local college, and has added the roles of producer and actor to his already full plate.

"Shep's been gone for a long time now," said Ricky, "but I think about him often. He literally taught me to take responsibility and to double-check not only my actions, but also the actions of those around me. Whether they realize it or not, my brothers really did me a favor when they got Shep. He was a good horse. He taught me to ride, and I mean really ride, and I am extremely proud to have known him."

www.rickylynngregg.com

Ricky Lynn Gregg Fan Club
P.O. Box 1600
Huntington, WV 25716

*Ricky Lynn Gregg at about age ten, ponying
one of the Gregg's ranch horses.*

The Wilkinsons

"It's been a long time since country music has seen an act as fresh and as exuberant as the Wilkinsons. Steve, Amanda and Tyler are the dad, daughter and son combo that's been sent to reinject country music with glistening harmonies, solid lyrics and soaring vocals. Genuine has become a word that sets off warning bells, so abused as it's been in our modern world. But if there is a word to capture what sets this trio apart in today's country music landscape, it's most definitely genuine."
Countrystars.com

Genuine is definitely what you get with this family trio. The Canadian-born Wilkinsons have one of the most amazing success stories in country music. Dad Steve, daughter Amanda, and son Tyler, received more nominations, awards and honors in their first two years on the scene than most artists garner in a lifetime. In 1999 alone, they were nominated for everything from the Country Music Association's Horizon Award and Vocal Group of the Year, to the Academy of Country Music's nominations for Single of the Year, and Top Vocal Duo or Group—well over twenty nominations! The three-some have also taken home a remarkable five Canadian Country Music awards (Single of the Year, Album of the Year, Song of the Year, Group or Duo of the Year, and the Wrangler Rising Star Award) and four Big Country awards (Best Vocal Group/Duo of the Year, Single of the Year, Video of the Year and Album of the Year).

The Wilkinsons have always done things their way. The family group, known for their sweet harmonies and fresh-scrubbed image, call what other acts might describe as a grueling tour schedule, as an opportunity. Not only have they savored being able to see so much of the country, but they credit their daily shows with a definite sharpening of their abilities. "Being on the road has strengthened our voices, and given us range and tones we never had before," says Amanda. "That really helped when we came in to record. We were able to focus and stretch, both vocally and with our music. We had a confidence that we didn't have before."

As much as they enjoy touring, when this family is off the road, you are as likely to find them in the horse barn, as you are at home. As you will see, horses, and in particular, a little colt who was born on Father's Day, are a family activity that helps them keep their career in perspective and their family priorities in order.

To talk about their interest in horses, the Wilkinsons graciously invited me to their beautiful log home on the outskirts of Nashville. Once there, I found a very warm and close family who obviously love each other, and their horses, very much.

"I remember when I was eight years old in Canada and there was a horse drawn milk wagon that came by our house every morning," said Steve. "The horse's name was Ted and I'd go out and give him carrots. This horse knew the milk route. He knew where to start and when to stop. Ted would just pull the wagon to the next house, and he'd stop and wait for the milk to be delivered and then he'd take himself on to the next house. The milkman would take several deliveries from the wagon at one time and cut through people's yards and this old dapple gray horse would just follow down the street and do his thing, It was amazing to watch. Later on, I had a paper route and the route took me by the creamery and I'd go visit Ted after he retired. His retirement was such a big deal that it made our local Belleville paper. I think that whole experience made me realize at an early age that horses were very, very special."

Steve lived on a farm on the shores of Lake Ontario. His dad had work horses and in the winter, Steve would help his dad take the horses out on the lake to cut ice.

"I can tell you I have a whole lot more good to say about a work horse than I do about a tractor," said Steve.

Steve and his wife, Kris, later broke horses for a friend near Calgary.

"I had this friend who had a lot of horses. We'd end up riding out there so much that we got to be pretty good. He'd eventually just tell us, 'Listen I've got fifteen or twenty green ones that need miles. Can you come out and ride?' I'd help gather them in and saddle them and put the bridles on. I learned so much about the individual personalities of horses there and I really became fascinated with them."

It was repeatedly hearing stories from those times that initially got a young Amanda and Tyler interested in riding. While still living in Canada, Amanda would spend time with a friend who had hunter/jumpers and who rode Dressage, and Tyler vividly recalls his first trail ride when he was five.

"I've always loved horses," said Amanda. "Hearing the stories that my dad tells makes me appreciate what horses are all about. I learned to ride when I was eight, but I also learned that it's good to ride, but the caring for them part is important too."

Even though the entire family, including Kris and younger daughter, Kiaya, have a passion for horses, it wasn't until a few years ago that the Wilkinsons had the opportunity to get into horses as a family.

"Being in music, it started out that we were going into the horses to take the stress away," said Tyler, "but we all loved it so much that it grew to be so much more than that for all of us."

"It's like we are addicted," interjected Amanda. "There is such a personality to them."

"Other than scuba diving," Tyler added, "being involved with the horses is one thing we can all do together."

And together, the Wilkinsons are definitely a family. There is a strong sense of ease in their togetherness. They are well attuned to each other, continually interrupting and seemlessly finishing sentences that other family members begin, laughing with each other

through the process. The day I visited, their herd included four horses: Cherokee, Amanda's paint; Lakota, a quarter-type mare; Willow,
her two-month-old colt; and Sashaw, a buckskin Quarter Horse mare
that had just been brought into the family the week before.

"We do a lot of stuff together and horses are sort of an extension
of what we do—who we are as a family," said Steve. "There is so
much enjoyment that we get out of certain hobbies, but horses tend
to be more than a hobby because there is a responsibility to them
and, for me at least, they give me a real sense of peace. When I am
out there and around them at sunset. . .I mean it doesn't get any better than that."

Steve said every night that they are not on the road, the entire
family can be found at the barn. If Kris and Kiaya stay home from a
road trip, they too, spend their free moments with the horses. In fact,
Kiaya just began showing, and received a second place ribbon her
first time out.

"Kiaya is a great rider," said Amanda. "It's like she has Velcro on
her butt."

"It was incredible," added Steve. "We were out on the road, so
we didn't get to see it, but I am so proud of her."

The horses have been especially good for Kris.

"Being around the horses has been a tremendous growth process
for her," commented Steve. "She had a bad fall from a horse when
she was pregnant with Amanda and had been terrified ever since. It's
been great to watch her conquer that and grow to love and enjoy the
horses as much as the rest of us do."

The Wilkinson's first colt was born on Father's Day, 2001, and
quickly forged a special bond with Tyler.

"The baby is so friendly, he's a real people horse," said Steve.
"The mare, Lakota, has a real good disposition and that's obviously
been passed on to the colt, but I think it's because we spend a lot of
time out there with them, too. They learn to trust people."

"I can just go in and sit down beside him in the stall when he's
lying down, and it's just incredible," said Tyler. "It's just the best feeling. I can't wait to watch him grow up."

The colt, named Willow by the Wilkinson's fan club, has become
a true family project.

Steve said, "Lakota is quiet and calm, intelligent. It's been so neat to see the stages of her letting go with the colt. I can't get nearly enough time watching them. The first few weeks she kept her body between us and the colt."

"Then after a while, she was like, 'go take a look, it's OK,'" said Amanda.

"Her letting go, it's all part of the bonding experience with her and the colt and us. It's so great to be a part of it," added Tyler.

"It was so neat when Lakota finally said to us, 'I trust you,'" this from Amanda.

"I've found that trust is a gained issue both ways between you and a horse. I'm not sure people actually own horses. I think it's more that they agree to be with you," finished Steve.

And trust, along with confidence and experience, are things that the Wilkinsons and their horses are gaining daily.

"This week we were cleaning out Cherokee's feet," Steve explained. "Amanda couldn't get him to pick his foot up, so I reached down and helped bring it up, and Amanda cleaned it out and Chris came right around and put in some antibiotic. Everybody's got a job. We're a team together with our horses."

But being a member of team Wilkinson means caring for others, no matter whether you are horse or human.

"One time I was longing Cherokee in a round pen," said Amanda. "He was going around and around and around and there was a patch of straw with a little spot of mud underneath it. Cherokee stepped in it and slipped and fell and landed on my leg. I got up just in time and he looked at me with the saddest expression, and I could tell how bad he felt. He thought he'd hurt me. He was looking at me and his ears were down and he was so concerned for me—almost like a dog would be. I stood there and talked to him, and I said, 'It's okay, I'm fine, don't worry about it. You didn't mean it.' And after a little while he was okay. He just gave this big sigh and you could just see and feel his relief that I was okay."

"Cherokee can be stubborn, but he knows he's Amanda's horse. He looks after her," explained Tyler.

The Wilkinsons say they plan to look after their horses for the rest of their lives.

"Not too long after Willow was born, we came back from being away on the road for about two weeks," said Steve. "We went out to the barn and Kiaya had a halter on the little one and a rope around his butt and she's leading him around. I said, 'Good Lord how long have you been doing that?' And she said, 'Well, I've been doing it for about ten minutes a night while you've been gone.' And now he's following us all around like we're his family."

"And we are," added Amanda. "Watching this colt, I've learned patience and I'm learning to deal with him on his level, which isn't necessarily my level, so it's sometimes a stretch. He pushes me and then learns he can't. I guess it's kind of like raising a kid."

"I want to be with this horse when he's like twenty," said Tyler. "Wouldn't that be incredible, to be there for the whole thing, his whole life?"

For the Wilkinsons, their horses are truly a part of their family.

As Steve puts it, "It's a matter of possession versus companion. To some people, horses are possessions. To us, our horses are definitely our companions. They are part of our routine, our family unit. They are like our dogs, irreplaceable. I can't imagine our life without them. They have brought so much more peace and joy and unity to us than we had before. Like I said about the old milk horse, Ted. Horses are very, very special."

www.wilkinsonsonline.com

The Wilkinsons Fan Club
P.O. Box 128365
Nashville, TN 37212

Tyler, Amanda and Steve with Willow and Lakota.

Kris, Kiaya, Tyler, Amanda, and Steve with Sashaw.

Perfect Stranger

"This man [lead singer Steve Murray], is simply an electrifying vocalist."
Bob Oermann, *Music Row Magazine*

The band Perfect Stranger began in the early 1980s in a living room in East Texas. Founding members Shayne Morrison and Richard Raines didn't know it at the time, but they had just formed one of the hottest road bands in the Texas/Oklahoma/Louisiana region. But it wasn't until the addition of lead singer Steve Murray in 1992, however, that the band found its legs. Steve added a serious country presence, along with a voice that was obviously the real thing. In late 1994, Perfect Stranger released a single, Ridin' the Rodeo, *on a small independent record label. Amazingly enough, Country Music Television picked up the accompanying video. It was a major accomplishment for an independent act, a strong indication of the level of excitement this East Texas group was generating. A second release in February 1995,* You Have the Right to Remain Silent, *jumped onto the* Billboard *charts, eventually landing in the top-five. The group signed with Curb records later that spring.*

Steve Murray is a real life cowboy who grew up surrounded by horses and who actually made money for a time as a rodeo team roper. These days, he balances being Perfect Stranger's on-stage anchor and lead vocalist, with life on the horse ranch his family owns. Steve credits his ease in dealing with the many people he comes in contact with as a star of country music, to the many horses he's been privileged to know throughout his life.

Steve Murray was born in the small East Texas town of Crockett. His grandparents were farmers and ranchers, but for some reason his father moved away from that and became a truck driver.

"My dad chose the steady job," said the easy-going singer. "But every weekend he would carry us back to the ranch. We had a little house in town and we had a place on the ranch—a home place—I call it. Every weekend we'd go all day long and kind of camp out. We were always outdoors."

As soon as Steve was old enough to sit on a horse, he was riding. In fact, he's been riding so long, he doesn't even remember learning to ride.

"The first horse that was really mine," said Steve, "was a little Shetland my dad bought me. She was a little paint mare called Misty. Meanest little thing in the world. When I decided I wanted to ride I'd have to get out there and chase her around. I mean, it was a pretty small patch and I'd have to chase that thing around for two to three hours before I could finally get her hemmed up so's I could get on her. And that taught me a lot. If you want to ride a horse, you've got to keep them in a stall."

When Steve was about twelve, he had the opportunity to raise his first colt, a big gray Quarter Horse gelding he named Pokey.

"This colt grew up to be a beautiful horse," said Steve. "I trained him myself and showed him in western pleasure and halter and won a bunch of stuff. When I was in 4-H, I carried him to all the 4-H shows and I showed him at the Houston Livestock show one year."

About that same time, Steve's dad had a good friend that turned the elder Murray on to cutting horses. Virtually very weekend when Steve was young, Steve's dad and his friend would get together to cut and pen cows, while Steve and his two younger brothers would be allowed to turn back. For whatever reason, other than helping their dad, Steve and his brothers weren't into the faster riding activities—contests such as the traditional game events of barrel racing and pole bending, or the rougher cattle work—preferring to stick to the halter and pleasure classes at local shows. But as Steve grew older, the roping bug bit big time.

"I didn't have anything to rope off of, so I decided I wanted to teach Pokey to do that as he was out of a Sugar Bars mare and an Enterprising King stud horse and was really bred for cattle work," explained Steve. "If you've ever been around horses, you know you don't ask too much physically of a horse like Pokey—a horse that you western pleasure ride on or that you show in halter.

"Well, me and Pokey fought and fought and fought one another about this ropin' thing. With ropin', it all starts in the box. You rope and the horse has to run to the cow. You rope the cow and if you're headin' you turn off and it's tough on a horse that's never been asked to do something like that. Pokey finally had to go to work and all of a sudden he's blowin' up in the box and rearing up and stuff like that. It was tough to get him out of that. This is an older horse now, we're talking about a seven-year-old. . .six. . .seven-year-old, kind of set in his ways. I'd bring him back down to the headin' box over and over and over again and put him in there and settle him down and score some cows on him and after a while, he was all right. The ropin' was something that was being forced on him that he didn't know anything about, but finally he just ended up and made a great rope horse. That's why he was so special because you could just do anything off him.

"When we finally retired Pokey, my brother's youngest son, he rode him quite a bit," added Steve. "Pokey was crippled by then. And when I say crippled I mean he moved slow, from arthritis and stuff. Pokey was in his late twenties when he died on our place out there in Crockett. That horse was one of my best friends and I still miss him every single day."

Steve says that horses are much like people to him.

"Horses, like people, all have different attitudes. They wake up and they feel, like us, good one day, cranky the next. A horse doesn't feel the same way everyday and neither do we. Sometimes a horse feels like doing something and sometimes he doesn't. What that taught me is that sometimes horses, like people, need an attitude adjustment every now and then. Little kids need a firm hand every now and then. I was raised that if I did something wrong, I kinda got punished, and you can do the same thing with a horse to an extent. Not to be too rough on a horse, but when you ask them to do something, if you're not firm enough, they know you're not firm enough and they know they can get away with anything. And they'll run all over you.

"I think coming from a good country background, you are basically a good person inside," said Steve thoughtfully. "All of our violence and all that we have with young kids, I really don't think people or kids that grew up with horses and that way of life have that kind of problem. I may be wrong. But that is my opinion. A horse is not like a motorcycle where you can park it and then you go put gas in it. A horse has to be fed before the family, he has to be fed even before you eat. That's the bottom line. The kids that are in trouble, they have no responsibility. A horse is definitely a big responsibility."

Today Steve says there are twenty-five to thirty head of Quarter Horses at the 5M Ranch. If he's been out on the road with the band, the first thing Steve does when he gets back is walk around and look at everything, especially taking notice of any new babies on the ground. Steve also keeps his training skills honed.

"I've got two I'm working with right now. . .two-year-olds. They are big stout geldings and, like people, they're as different as night and day. One of them is at the top of the class. He is so smart it is not even funny. And the other one, he kinda stumbles over his own feet every now and then, and he is a little bit slow to learn some things."

You don't spend more than a few minutes with Steve before you find that he thoroughly enjoys the time he spends riding and training.

"Music lets me do what I'm really good at," he said. "The singing and playing, that's really a hobby to me, it's fun and I love doing it, love meeting all the people, but when I get back to the house and to the horses, that's what I feel I'm really good at."

According to Steve, the best part of his life with Perfect Stranger is all the traveling that the band gets to do and all the different people they have had the opportunity to meet. He particularly enjoys seeing different countries. So far, they have toured in Switzerland and Japan, and performed on several cruises.

"The reality is, I'm a kid from Crockett, Texas. There's like four-or five hundred people there," said Steve. "I know people that live there their whole lives and never go anywhere. I've gotten to do some things that a lot of my friends wouldn't ever dream of doing, or they only dream of doing."

Steve added that he felt that horses helped prepare him for the wide variety of people and places he's experienced in the music business.

"By riding a lot of different horses, chances are you've seen what that horse is doing somewhere before. I've rode so many of them, I've had them do everything they can possibly do. They buck with you, they trip and fall with you, they love on you, they work with you. How else would a country kid from Crockett, Texas feel comfortable talking with a fan in Japan, or eating dinner with a promoter in Europe? Every time I meet a new person, they're gonna say something or do something that tells me something about them. Then, like with the horses, I can say, 'Oh, yeah, I really can find common ground with this person. I know this type. I've seen this before.' And it gives me a start with them."

The fame hasn't changed Steve, but he says that people react differently to him at home now.

"They treat me like I'm something that I'm not," he said, with a shake of his head. "Like my friends, or some kids come up, 'Mr. Murray, how're ya doing,' and I've always been just Steve, you know. But for some reason since I'm doing what I am, and I'm on the radio every now and then, I guess that carries you to a whole different level with people. Once in a while I see their point, but it's strange, very strange to me. The horses, they know I'm still just Steve, so they're a lot smarter than people in that respect."

In a perfect world, according to Steve, everyone would have a horse.

"It'll bring something good to your life," he said. "Having a horse can't do anything but improve your life. If someone were thinking about getting into horses, I'd say, 'What's been holding you back, what's stopping you?' There's always a way if someone wants something bad enough.

"I think bein' around a horse kinda puts you at peace," Steve concluded. "When we're on the road, you know, I love meeting all the people but I'm really kind of a quiet. . .a little bit of a shy person. So to me, there's nothing like riding a good horse through the woods by yourself. It's just so peaceful. It puts my feet back on the ground is what it does. I've rode so many of them. What's it's taught me is that none of them are alike and that every day, every horse, every person is different, but we all have some things that are similar. If you can find that similarity, you can get along with that person no matter who or what or where they are. I couldn't imagine my life when I was a kid, growing up without horses around. And I can't imagine my life now without horses. It just wouldn't be life."

www.curb.com

Steve Murray with horses from the 5M Ranch.

Brad Paisley

"When Randy Travis came along he brought back enthusiasm for traditional country music. Then more recently, Alan Jackson has reminded fans of how great traditional country music is. And now I am counting on you to carry on the tradition and make folks sit up and listen to what good country music should sound like."
George Jones (from a letter written to Brad Paisley and read at his Grand Ole Opry induction February 19, 2001)

Brad Paisley is country. In his life and in his music. Especially his music. Many people in the country music community, refer to Paisley as the torchbearer for traditional country music. But Brad will be the first to tell you he's led a charmed life, that everything just seems to fall into place for him. What he doesn't say, although it gradually becomes evident, is that his run of good fortune has been enhanced enormously by hard work, astounding musical talent and a clear, unwavering vision of where he wants to go.

Brad was born and raised in Glen Dale, West Virginia, a Mayberry-type town with a population of just 1,800. When he was eight, his grandfather, a night shift railroad worker who spent his afternoons playing guitar, gave him a gift: a Sears Danelectro Silvertone guitar with an amp in the case. The gift would change Brad's life.

Fast-forward twenty years. Brad Paisley's critically acclaimed debut album, Who Needs Pictures, *was certified platinum. The album produced two number one hits, both of which Paisley co-wrote. One of them was the smash* He Didn't Have To Be, *which many music writers, country radio announcers and fellow musicians are already calling a career song. Brad was also the most-nominated and most-awarded new country artist of the year in 2000. He tied Faith Hill for the most nominations (six) at the Country Music Association awards, and took home the coveted Horizon Award.*

With a heavy tour schedule, recording sessions, meetings with his business advisors, and requests for interviews constantly coming right and left, Brad finds spending time with his horse, Pal, the best way to get away from it all.

Brad Paisley has been around other people's horses all his life, but it wasn't until the last few years that he had the opportunity to own one of his own. We met for the interview in a back room of the new Country Music Hall of Fame, a gorgeous, sweeping architectural tribute to everything country. I caught Brad between interviews for several Country Music Television programs and he quickly warmed to one of his favorite subjects, horses.

"The whole thing about horses, I'm totally into all of it. Horses, and my one horse in particular, have taught me so much," said Brad. "But the one big thing I've learned I'd have to say is friendship. This horse has really taught me what it means to be a friend."

The horse that Brad values so much for friendship is a palomino Quarter Horse gelding named Palomar. And Brad realized right away that for him, having a horse is much better than having a dog.

"I don't have any other pets. I just have one pet and it's this horse and it's perfect because I'm not around a lot. You can't be away from a dog for a week or two at a time on a regular basis," he commented. "This horse—I call him Pal because he really is my pal—he's such a great friend. [The name] Pal fits for his color and for the friendship we have. A horse, they're definitely herd oriented, and mine's got a buddy to hang with when I'm on the road, so he doesn't care too much when I'm gone."

The buddy is a ten-year-old gelding named Whiskers. Whiskers and Pal really are best buddies, eating and grazing and dozing together in the sun. At least that's the plan until Brad comes off the road and heads to the barn. Then Pal heads straight for Brad.

"Pal's the kind of horse that if I show up in the pasture, if he's on the far side, he could be several acres away," said Brad. "But if he sees me, he'll start coming and he'll walk all the way across that field just to stick his nose in my chest and get rubbed. And maybe I've been gone a couple of weeks, but he doesn't hold a grudge. He's my friend unconditionally, and always, he's just glad to see me."

Brad, who is just as personable off-stage as he is on, became interested in owning a horse a few years ago after a friend described some of the benefits.

"I took some English [riding] lessons and quickly decided that western was more my thing," laughed Brad. "This relationship is my first as a horse owner, so I'm learning a lot. I've been around horses quite a bit but never owned one myself until now. Even though people in my family would have horses that I was around, they were never my horse, and that makes a big difference. You never realize that until you actually have a horse of your own."

Pal obviously doesn't care where Brad's single is on the charts, or how many people came to his last concert. It doesn't matter to Pal if the artwork on the CD cover has to be redone or if Brad and his crew have to drive eight hundred miles to the next show. Pal likes Brad simply for the time Brad spends with him. It's a relationship that has enhanced both their lives.

"One thing that Pal has taught me is that it's nice for me to have a friend like a horse where I can come and go as my road schedule allows," said Brad. "When I am home, though, I spend almost all my free time out there at this farm where I keep Pal. He's just the best and we've really bonded in so many ways. I was so lucky. I got such a good horse my first time out. Pal's got a really, really good disposition. He's very calm. And he's very laid back."

According to Brad, Pal, six, and his buddy Whiskers, ten, have been together for many years. But it never ceases to amaze Brad that the minute Brad steps into the pasture, Pal leaves Whiskers and comes to him.

"Having my own horse now, having had him for a couple of years, I've come to know it is a relationship like no other," said Brad. "Here's this 1,300 pound animal who relies on you to some degree. Not only that, he lets me know in so many ways that he really is happy I am there with him. That kind of relationship—contrast it with the absolute opposite spectrum of the music world that I live in every day—the horse part of my world has enhanced my life in a way that I never thought that it would."

For Brad, spending time with Pal is a way to forget the daily pressures his career brings. It is a way for him to get some much needed quiet time, to organize his thoughts, and to enjoy the solitude that only a horse and a country road can bring.

"When you're riding a horse, you are not thinking about your day job, or your work, or your career," said Brad. "You're just thinking at all times about where you're headed on this horse and where you're going next. You're anticipating every move that horse makes, especially with Pal as he's still being trained. He's a six-year-old, but I guess in some ways they're always being trained. This is a situation, though, where at six he's got a lot to learn yet. He's actually forgotten a lot of the things he did learn, because I haven't been there as much in the recent months as I would have liked, or as much as I will be in the spring when I can work with him more."

Brad says he really looks forward to his time with his friend.

"For me," he said, "the anticipation of riding for a couple of hours just puts my mind in a place so totally away from the music business. I just can't tell you how nice that is, or how important it is. I totally forget about anything that has to do with music, you know? I love what I do, I love making music, but everyone needs a break now and then. Anyone who has or has had a horse probably is very aware of what I'm talking about. Any problems, all problems in your life are gone for those couple of hours. It's impossible almost to really ride a horse and focus on anything else. It adds a ton of balance to my life. I need that balance and nothing else but horses, and this horse in particular, Pal, my pal, delivers it for me. He is my best friend."

www.bradpaisley.com

Brad Paisley Fan Club
P.O. Box 121113
Nashville, TN 37212

Brad Paisley competing in a celebrity cutting.

Lynn Anderson

"Lynn Anderson may not have promised us a rose garden but she has given music lovers around the world much, much more. Lynn Anderson is the definition of legend."
countrycharts.com

One of the top-ranked female vocalists in any genre, Lynn Anderson's strong, husky vocals have literally generated too many awards to mention. She is considered one of the finest entertainers in the world and is often called "The Great Lady of Country Music."
Lynn has performed for five U.S. Presidents, the Queen of England, HRH Charles Prince of Wales, Princes Rainier and Albert of Monaco, and King Hussan; and has been featured on The Tonight Show, The Carol Burnett Show, Solid Gold, Good Morning America *and three Bob Hope specials. She has acted in episodes of* Starsky and Hutch, Country Gold *and in an NBC Movie of the Week. Lynn has also starred in her own CBS television special.*
Born in Grand Forks, North Dakota, and raised in California, Lynn's love of country music can be attributed to her mother, song-writing great Liz Anderson. Liz composed such smash hits as The Fugitive *for Merle Haggard.*
As a teenager, Lynn entered a singing contest. By the time she was twenty, Lynn had been with a national recording company for

three years, and had scored a string of hits. When Lynn signed a contract with Lawrence Welk, she became the only country performer featured on national television at the time.

In 1970, Lynn moved to Nashville and began turning out a stream of well-received recordings. About this time, Lynn entered the studio to record Joe South's (I Never Promised You a) Rose Garden. *What emerged was a bit of magic. The song climbed to the top of the country charts, cracked the top-five on the pop charts and transformed the young singer into a national celebrity.*

Rose Garden *made Lynn an international superstar, and brought home a Grammy for Best Female Vocal Performance of the Year. Lynn was also named Female Vocalist of the Year by the Academy of Country Music and the Country Music Association, as well as being named* Record World's *Female Artist of the Decade.*

Her success was followed by even more hits, including Under the Boardwalk, *and* Top of the World, *which won the Country Music Association's Song of the Year. To date, Lynn has had eight number one singles, earned sixteen gold albums, and won virtually every award available to a female artist.*

Lynn is also an avid horsewoman with sixteen national championships, eight world championships and several celebrity championships under her belt. Her most recent wins include the National Chevy Truck Cutting Horse Champion, 1999; American U.S. Open Invitational Champion, 2000; and the National Cutting Horse Association Champion, 1999. While Lynn has many equestrian honors from childhood on, she is proudest of her accomplishments as a breeder of fine Quarter Horses and Paints.

There must be a law somewhere that says that you can't write a book about country music artists and their horses and not include Lynn Anderson. From her earliest days she has been passionate, and wildly successful, about both; and is a contender close to attaining two lifelong goals, being inducted into the Country Music Hall of Fame and the Cowgirl Hall of Fame.

"I started singing not too long after I started riding," said Lynn. "Music and horses are both lifelong passions and I am equally as

serious about my horses as I am about my singing. I've been fortunate throughout my life in that I've been able to blend them."

Lynn was all of eight years of age when her parents gave in to
her ceaseless requests that they move to a ranch where she could
have a horse.

"We moved to Sacramento," she recalled, "and got about four
acres with twenty acres surrounding it that we could use, so this was
my big horse ranch." And, to complete the move, Lynn's parents
bought her a horse.

"His name was Apache, and he and the saddle and bridle and
breast collar and blanket cost a total of eighty-five dollars. Apache
was the ugliest paint Mustang you ever saw," laughed Lynn. "But
that horse taught me a lot of good stuff about horsemanship, namely
how to fall off and get back on." Lynn said it took several weeks of
concentrated effort before she could coax Apache out of a walk,
kicking all the way. "And once I got him trotting, he would trot faster
and faster, and faster. It was like Calamity Jane, you know, you get
bouncing on your butt until you just bounce too high to come back
down and land in the saddle, so I'd land on the ground and have to
catch him and drag myself back up."

Lynn finally learned to ride well enough to urge Apache into a
gallop.

"Of course, then he ran straight back to the barn. But those were
lessons that you had to learn," she said. "I had to walk a couple of
weeks before I could trot. He didn't crawl, or we'd have done that
first! Apache was a mess and ugly as sin but I never will forget him."

Soon after Lynn learned to ride Apache, her grandparents, who
bred Tennessee Walking horses, sent her a palomino Walking horse
stallion named Dakota Chief. By the time she was nine, Lynn had
won a reserve championship in Horsemanship at the Cow Palace in
San Francisco.

"My trainers when I was a child are all in the Hall of Fame now,"
she commented. "Don Dodge, Matlock Rose. . .those were people I
worked with when I was a kid, when I was training to ride when I
was nine, ten, eleven years old. They are all people that I still know,
except now they are legends in the cutting horse industry."

Lynn went on to win championships with Tennessee Walking

Horses, Paints, Palominos, and American Saddlebreds; and has ridden Paso Finos, Peruvian Pasos, and Olympic caliber jumpers. Out of all the horses Lynn has been involved with throughout her life, she says there are several major standouts.

"There's a mare I had named Doc Starlight who is in the Hall of Fame in the National Cutting Horse Association," explained Lynn. "Her first baby was named Gray Starlight after my son, Gray, and her first daughter was named Bunny Starlight after my daughter, Bunny. Gray Starlight has gone on to be one of the top cutting horse stallions in the world. The Doc Starlight line is now a very famous line in the cutting horse world and I'm very proud of that because these horses are kind of like my children."

Another favorite of Lynn's is a Paint mare called Delta.

"Delta was the first world champion cutting horse that was a Paint. She was world champion four times in the Paint world, but she was the first Paint to be in the Hall of Fame with the Quarter Horses in the National Cutting Horse Association," Lynn said.

Delta was given to Lynn as a gift.

"At the time, I kept my horses at Pear Tree Quarter Horse Farm in Fairview, Tennessee. And the owner of the farm, Mr. Price, was one of the founders of the National Cutting Horse Association. Mr. Price let me play with this beautiful Paint mare, Delta, and when I got married, he gave her to me as a wedding gift."

Lynn developed Delta as the foundation mare of a strong line of Paint progeny that includes Delta Flyer, Delta Doc O' Lena, and Delta Dawn, all national or world champions in their own right.

"Delta was very special just because of what she was—her parents were both Quarter Horses and she came out with spots," said Lynn. "She was absolutely gorgeous. She would look at you and you could tell that she had been hurt very badly at some point in her life. Her tongue was all scar tissue except for about an inch, and the reason she would work her heart out for me is because I never pulled on her mouth. I never jerked her, I just let her go because she knew everything so much better than I did. She was doing it all on her own so all I had to do was be a passenger and not get in her way."

Lynn and Delta won the Dixie National together when they were both seven months pregnant. "It was one of those things where I was at home and all my other horses were out on the road. Everybody I knew was out showing and everybody was having fun except the two old pregnant girls sitting at home," said Lynn. "So I drug Delta out, and we went to Jackson, Mississippi, and we won the non-Pro class and then we won the open cutting, and we were both big and fat and pregnant. That was Delta Flyer that she was carrying and I was carrying Gray Stream so we had a lot of progeny going there.

"These mares, Doc Starlight and Delta, were both cutting horses," said Lynn. "Both of them had a different style, but they had the same huge eye, and huge heart, and a special quietness—like a quiet intelligence—and you know that these horses when they look at you are looking right at you, right into your soul. When you see pictures of people swimming with dolphins, people don't often think that horses are intelligent like that but they are. They can look into your eyes and they see your heart. They know through your hands how you're going to treat them."

Even though several of the horses closest to Lynn's heart are national and world champion mares that founded her current breeding program, it is probably a little Quarter Horse gelding named Skipster's Chief, who Lynn is most proud of.

"I first saw Chief at the Indiana State Fair and there was a six-year-old little girl riding him. He was a chestnut horse with four white socks and a big blaze and a flaxen mane and tail. This fair was an absolutely huge place, hundreds of people, and here was this little tiny, tiny girl toodling around in and out of all these horses, racing around the ring and warming up and stuff," said Lynn in amazement. "This horse was a baby sitter. He was like holding her hand and taking care of her. Chief knew that he had this little precious treasure on his back and he went beautifully for her."

Lynn had been looking for a horse for her children to ride and felt that Chief was perfect for the job. He even had the same name as one of her first horses, the Tennessee Walking Horse her grandparents had given her.

"So that's the horse my children learned to ride on and since then he's probably taught a couple of hundred kids to learn to ride," said Lynn. "He was a doll."

Lynn later donated Chief to Animaland, a therapeutic riding program for handicapped kids located in Franklin, Tennessee. At the time, it was one of the first programs of its kind in the country. Chief became the poster horse for NARAH, the National Association for Riding and the Handicapped.

"He was so good," said Lynn. "Kids would shimmy up his legs. They could run underneath him and hang on his tail, which might have been good or might have been bad, but they trusted him so much. They'd probably use those practices around another horse and get kicked, but Chief was so gentle and so wonderful that you could not help but love him. Chief spent a good ten or twelve years being scratched and rubbed by kids all day every day and you can't ask for a better life than that. He impacted the lives of so many kids in a really positive way. I am really proud to have had a part in that."

Chief is now buried at Animaland, but before he died, he was immortalized as a plastic model horse by the Breyer Company. Another of Lynn's horses, Lady Phase, was also chosen by Breyer as their model for "the perfect Quarter Horse."

Of all her equine pursuits, Lynn loves the breeding part of things the most.

"Mares are the most important part of the breeding program because stallions can breed a couple of hundred mares, but the very best of his crop is what you get is from one special mare. I think a lot of people in the horse business will agree with me that eighty to ninety percent of what you get in a baby is from the mare," said Lynn. "Obviously you have to choose the right stallion to breed to which is why I am so proud of being able to research the bloodlines and figure out what's going to cross and what's going to work.

"Take Delta," she illustrated. "We went to [the Quarter Horse] Peppy San Badger with her—he's known as Little Peppy—but we used him because he's double bred Leo breeding and Leo has an excessive white gene. I had a good feeling that crossed together they would make a nice Paint baby, and they did. I've studied bloodlines for a long time and that's the kind of research you have to do if you're going to get as far into the horse business as breeding."

Lynn currently has ten horses, all of them sons and daughters of mares she rode to national or world championships.

"I had four really, really, good mares and they are the product of a lifetime of riding and loving horses," concluded Lynn. "I've always loved horses—you develop a really strong bond with them. They look through your eyes and see your soul. They look right into your heart, and I don't know another animal on Earth that can do that."

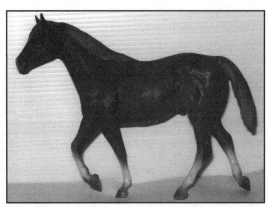

www.lynnanderson.net

Lynn Anderson
International Fan Club
P.O. Box 90454
Charleston, SC 29410

Above right: the Breyer horse model of Skipster's Chief.
Above: Lynn and Delta in a cutting competition.

Charlie Daniels

"Few individuals have symbolized the South in popular culture as directly and indelibly as Charlie Daniels."
Encyclopedia of Southern Culture

Like Texas, Charlie Daniels is part Western and part Southern. His signature bullrider hat and belt buckle, life on his Twin Pines Ranch, his love of horses, cowboy lore, rodeo heroes, Western movies, and Louis L'Amour novels, identify him as a Westerner. The son of a timberman and a Southerner by birth, his music—rock, country, bluegrass, blues, and gospel—is completely Southern.

It's not so much his music as his values that have connected Charlie with millions of fans. For decades, he has refused to label his music as anything other than "Charlie Daniels Band music," music that is now sung at 4-H and scout camps, helped elect an American president, and been popularized in many radio formats.

After graduating from high school, Charlie, a talented guitar, fiddle and mandolin player, formed a rock band and hit the road. Enroute to California, Charlie stopped in Texas to record Jaguar, *an instrumental that was picked up for national distribution. Charlie then co-wrote* It Hurts Me, *which became the B side of an Elvis hit. Charlie also served as a musician on recording sessions, including the Bob Dylan albums* Nashville Skyline, New Morning, *and* Self

Portrait; *and Charlie eventually broke through with his own records. His rebel anthems* Long Haired Country Boy *and* The South's Gonna Do It *are well-known by fans of any genre.*

In 1979, Charlie delivered The Devil Went Down to Georgia, *which became a platinum single, topped country and pop charts, won a Grammy, earned three Country Music Association awards, became a cornerstone of the* Urban Cowboy *movie soundtrack and propelled Charlie's* Million Mile Reflections *album to triple platinum. By 1981, the Charlie Daniels Band had twice been voted the Academy of Country Music's Touring Band of the Year.*

Other platinum albums include Full Moon, Simple Man, *and* A Decade of Hits. *Charlie earned a Dove Award from the Gospel Music Association in 1994 for* The Door; *and* Amazing Grace: A Country Salute to Gospel, *a compilation album including Charlie's* Kneel at the Cross, *garnered a Grammy in 1995. In 1996 Charlie was honored with a boxed set of his classics, and his catalog now represents more than eighteen million units in sales.*

Charlie's annual Volunteer Jam concerts were the foundation for many of today's annual day-long music marathons, and featured a variety of artists. The Jams are often considered Charlie's most impressive contribution to Southern music. With an unerring instinct for the ties that bind people together, and a disgust for the intolerance and fear that do the opposite, Charlie Daniels has impacted the lives of everyday people everywhere.

In April 1998, two former U.S. presidents paid Charlie tribute when he won the Academy of Country Music's Pioneer Award. "In his time he's played everything from rock to jazz, folk to western swing, and honky-tonk to award-winning gospel," said former President Jimmy Carter. "In Charlie's own words, 'Let there be harmony. Let there be fun and twelve notes of music to make us all one.'"

Charles E. Daniels was born in Wilmington, North Carolina and doesn't remember learning how to ride.

"It's that much a part of me," he said. "We had farm animals as I was growing up, and some of the horses doubled as saddle horses and we rode those sometimes for work and other times for pleasure."

Although Charlie had a farm background and really enjoyed time he spent around horses, it wasn't until he was in his thirties that he bought a horse of his own. And although he is now heavily into Quarter Horses, the first horses Charlie bought were just horses that he liked, and included a Midnight Sun-type Tennessee Walking horse, an Arabian that had formerly been owned by a member of the Marshall Tucker Band, and several mixed breed horses.

"We had moved to Tennessee by then and I had to board the horses because we didn't have a place to keep them yet," he said. "In fact, the horses were the motivation to buy the farm. [Charlie's Twin Pines Ranch is located outside of Nashville.] The whole family rode then, including my wife and it was a large part of our life. Our family was always close, and riding and horses was an activity that we could all enjoy and do together."

Somewhere in the seventies, Charlie decided to make his life-long dreams of having a horse ranch a reality. Charlie bought some land with a double wide trailer on it and Charlie and a friend built the original barn (three stalls, tack room and paddock) themselves. He later added a new barn and an arena. Charlie had always wanted to rope, and by 1980 he had mostly "cowboy" horses, and with the addition of some beef cattle, the ranch was taking on a working aspect.

Thurman Mullins is a friend of Charlie's who came by to help out on the ranch in 1980 and has been there ever since. Shortly after Thurman's arrival, he sold Charlie's Arabians and Tennessee Walking horses for him and found a gelding called Major that Charlie learned to rope on.

"Major was a good solid horse for someone like me, who was just learning to throw a rope," said Charlie. "He wasn't flashy, but he was a hard worker and did well for me. So well, that I enjoyed it enough to stay in it all these years."

A few years later, Charlie found a registered Paint mare, Rialto's Lady, who soon became known around the barn as Fat Gal.

"Charlie would get out amongst the cattle and talk to old Fat Gal and she'd just do whatever he asked," said Thurman. "She was smart, and solid, and honest, and she was tough."

"Fat Gal was a big, chunky Paint horse and had a great personality," added Charlie. "She was a very loud white and dark chestnut, mix—she looked black and white from a distance. Fat Gal was only about 15.1, but very stout. Eleven or twelve hundred pounds and a number two shoe, so she was definitely big enough to carry me. She'd go all day long and work hard every minute. She had the mental capability to both head and heel, and do both well. We lost her a few years ago, at age twenty-two."

Fat Gal is buried on the Twin Pines Ranch.

"Any horse that serves me well is welcome to my pasture as long as they live, even after their riding days are over," commented Charlie. "I think you owe them something. Fat Gal was very welcome around the place even after we retired her."

When Fat Gal died, Thurman cut some hairs from her long, white tail.

"He sent the hairs to someone in Colorado who braided the hair very fine and made a watch chain. Thurman gave that watch chain to me and it is one of the nicest gifts I've ever received," said Charlie. "I'd never forget old Fat Gal, but this is a very nice way to remember her."

Freckles is another quarter-type horse who served Charlie well and who found a permanent home on the Twin Pines Ranch.

"Freckles was the kind of horse that we could load him up and take him down to a rodeo at the spur of the moment and win some money on him," said Charlie. "He was solid and consistent, that's the type of horse that makes me sit up and take notice, and that's the type of person I most admire, too. Just that steady effort to get the job done."

During the eighties and early nineties, Charlie had regular clinics and seminars at the ranch and Freckles became a big part of those clinics.

"If you were inexperienced or nervous, Freckles could read you," said Charlie, "he'd read you like a book and know exactly what you did and didn't know. But rather than take advantage of that, as some horses, and people, will, he's one of those rare horses that will actually teach you how to rope."

Freckles was almost thirty-five-years-old when he died this past year.

"He was in a field with two mares and a colt, and he started falling off some," Charlie said. "He earned his keep with us and he was happy, but after a certain age, we got to where we worried about him some."

Charlie loves the time he spends on his ranch and he loves the people and the horses who share that time with him.

"There is a whole code of ethics that these people, that true cowboys, abide by that includes honesty and honor, and that's something we don't see enough of anymore. That's the cowboy way and we like doing things that way at the ranch," said Charlie. "That's just how we run our business operations. And I enjoy it so much. I enjoy everything about it, the horses, the people, the cattle, being outdoors. I mean, I think I'd rather rope than have supper at the White House."

At one time, the Twin Pines Ranch had over forty Quarter Horse brood mares. Now the ranch runs a more manageable ten to twelve head, including a few new colts and a stallion. The smaller herd is part of Charlie's own prescription to decrease the stress of everyday life.

"I would highly advise anyone to just get on a horse and ride. It is that simple," he said. "There is something about riding a horse that is unique. There just is no other feeling like it. Once you get close to a horse mentally and emotionally, once you learn to trust them and they to trust you, you sit on their back and they've got their ears perked forward and there just is nothing better."

For many years, Charlie was heavily into both the competitive and working end of roping and heeling.

"I used to really enjoy going to see friends out West in the spring and help brand the calves, used to love loading up and going to a rodeo to rope and head and heel—I loved all of it. But I seem to be so much busier these days, I don't have the time I used to so I don't get to do things like that as much," said Charlie. "It's my goal to change that. I used to ride every day and I rode a lot at night. I'd go down to the arena and just ride. What a great feeling, just you and your horse, nothing else in the world exists for me during those times. Riding horses puts everything in life in perspective. It helps put your mind in order. I ride mostly for pleasure now. Horseback riding is second nature to me. To take care of a horse, put a saddle on one, and get on and ride out in the woods and fields, it is so much a part of my life that I can't imagine not having that. I can't think of a better way to spend leisure time than to sit on the back of a horse."

www.charliedaniels.com

Charlie Daniels Band Fan Club
14410 Central Pike
Mt. Juliet, TN 37122

Charlie and Freckles.

Charlie, Fat Gal, and one of her babies.

Tommy Shane Steiner

"A newcomer with a tug-at-your-heartstrings ballad. The lyrics really hit home this time of year."
Ray Randall, Jones Radio Network

Tommy Shane Steiner is a real cowboy with deep Texas roots, but he is just as comfortable in Hollywood hanging out on Sunset Strip as he is at home in Austin penning cattle with the rest of his family.

The Steiners are a tight knit family with a long and enriched tradition on the rodeo circuit. In fact, Tommy's great-grandfather, TC "Buck" Steiner, is a member of the Cowboy Hall of Fame and rode with many of the old legends, including Poncho Villa, Wild Bill Elliott, and Annie Oakley. Having known everyone from Gene Autry to Al Capone, a younger Tommy often wondered what his great-grandfather was thinking.

"He still thought of cars as being a buggy without the horse," Tommy jokes.

Tommy's grandfather, the late Tommy Steiner, is a member of both the Cowboy Hall of Fame and the Rodeo Hall of Fame, and was instrumental in turning rodeo into the all-encompassing entertainment it is today. Tommy and his younger brother, Sid, grew up traveling from one rodeo to the next with their 1973 World Champion bull riding father, Bobby, and barrel racing mother, Joleen. Like the three generations of Steiners before him, Sid followed suit and became a steer wrestler. But those close to the family say it is no surprise to them that the extroverted Tommy grew up to be an entertainer, especially as Bobby had recorded an independent album in 1974 on a label similar to one Chris LeDoux was on at the time.

Tommy's eclectic musical influences range from George Strait to Elton John, Alabama to Aerosmith, Limp Bizkit to Michael Jackson. Nevertheless, his debut release for RCA Records, Then Came the Night, *is definitely country. Tommy's growing league of fans will be horrified to learn that Tommy almost became a bull rider instead of having a singing career. Tommy credits a broncy ranch horse named Capîtan for throwing him into country music.*

Tommy Shane Steiner grew up with horses so ingrained in his life that he doesn't remember learning how to ride.

"There's a lot of pictures of me as a baby riding a horse," said Tommy. "Of course my parents are holding me in the saddle. They were putting me on horses from way before the time I could remember."

By the time Tommy was two years old, his dad was leading him around on one of their gentler horses. The Steiners ran 10,000 acres over two ranches in the Austin, Texas area, so finding a gentle horse for a toddler was not a problem. A few years later, Tommy and his younger brother, Sid, were riding in the grand entries at their Grandfather's rodeos.

"We'd follow along right behind my dad and they'd introduce him and they'd introduce us," said Tommy. "Of course by at least four I was riding by myself. I'd just follow my dad riding a horse around the arena."

Tommy remembers rodeo life as being a lot of fun.

"Growing up," he said, "it was like a circus. We just traveled around from rodeo to rodeo and my parents would try to have me at school on the school days. And during the summer, I was just gone."

When Tommy was home, he was on a ranch in Austin, Texas, but he could often be found working cattle on the nearby Bastrop ranch.

"We'd take off from school whenever we had to wean all the calves and stuff and we'd be gone two or three days. All my friends thought we were so lucky and I'd be like, 'Ahhh yeah, why don't you come out and spend the day?' They all thought it was like that movie, *City Slickers*. Like you just get to ride around and talk to your buddy, like 'Hey, it's great to be out here in the open range.' Meanwhile, my dad's going, 'What are you doing, talking??? Get over there, calves are breaking off the left.' And you know when you work for your family, there's not a whole lot of money involved."

Tommy's dad, Bobby, was the Professional Rodeo Cowboys Association world champion bull rider in 1973.

"Growing up in that environment, I always just assumed that I was going to be a bull rider just like Dad," Tommy said. "But Dad made it very clear that that was not going to be an option. He did not want my brother or me to be bull riders. I think he wasn't gonna be able to watch us get on every night, knowing the dangers and whatever."

That was fine with a young teen-aged Tommy. About that same time Bobby and Joleen decided their kids needed more of a home life, and Tommy and Sid found themselves involved baseball and football for a while instead. It provided much needed structure for the two boys, who tended to be on the wild side.

"I really think that if I'd stayed in that rodeo environment, that I'd be in prison now," said Tommy more than half-seriously.

"A lot of guys that rodeoed with my dad back in the old days, a lot of those guys said, 'Hey, I thought you'd be in prison by now.' So it's pretty amazing to them that I actually did something with my life."

There came a point in his late teens when Tommy felt he was old enough to make a career decision on his own.

"I really wanted to be a bull rider," said Tommy, with emphasis on the word really. "But my dad said, 'It's too late. You're too old to start riding bulls.' I disagreed with him. Of course, my dad started riding bulls when he was eleven, so at eighteen, nineteen, my dad was world champion."

Living on a ranch, Tommy had grown up riding calves and steers, but as anyone who's been around rodeo knows, it becomes a totally different situation when you bring a full-grown 1,500 to 2,000 pound bull into the picture. So Tommy split the difference.

"At a rodeo, they had this bucking machine and all these cow-boys who were steer wrestlers decided to get on," said Tommy. "It was so funny. You know steer wrestlers, they're not much of a bull rider. So they were all getting dumped off, and my brother, who is a steer wrestler, he rode it pretty good.

"Then Dad was like, 'Why don't you try it out?' I almost looked like I knew what I was doing, so after that I was like, 'Hey, I can do this.' But Dad was like, 'Hold on for a second. This is a bucking machine, all right? It doesn't have skin and it moves around and also, it's not going to hook your butt when you fall off.' But that bucking machine made me think I was good, and that's how I got interested in being a bull rider."

Tommy says he was probably eighteen or nineteen at that point. Soon after, he and his family were out on the ranch and were work-ing, penning cattle. Tommy was riding a huge, leggy sorrel Quarter Horse named Capîtan that day. And as Tommy remembers, his dad suggested he choose Capîtan for the day's work.

"I think my dad did this on purpose because later on I found out that this horse had bucked off several people," said Tommy. "Our whole family was out penning cattle that day. It was in the winter-time. It was cold. Usually when I think about penning cattle, I think about it being hot. But this was one of those times when it was brisk outside. We had some friends out helping us, and they'd turned some calves back.

"I was going out to catch this calf that had taken off at a dead run. And I'm just hauling after this calf. I mean this horse could run. And at a full run Capîtan just breaks and starts bucking. He was wanting to get out. He was just feeling good. We got out there and you know, he was a little jumpy all day, but when we were chasing after that calf, that's when he just wanted to have a little fun with me. Immediately I threw a stirrup. I was wearing tennis shoes or some-thing and was like, 'I'm gonna slip a foot through this stirrup if I keep trying to ride this one out.' And that's the reason you wear cowboy boots, to keep your foot from going through the stirrup. But at the time I was like, 'Ahhh, I'm gonna get hung up.' I mean this horse was bucking hard."

In the split second he had to think, Tommy gave serious thought to riding out the buck, but at the same time, he tried to find a better choice.

"It's amazing how many thoughts can go through your head in a split second. Because as I threw the stirrup it was like, 'OK, he's gonna buck,' because he just basically broke and blew straight up in the air. I actually had a little collision with the saddle horn on the first jump or two, which wasn't really all that fun. The thing is, you disregard that pain and focus what you need to do. Probably by the second or third hop I had weighed out all the options. Mainly, I'm way away from everybody. I'm thinking I'm so far away from everyone else that if I get hung up in the stirrup—I only had one left—this horse would drag me to death. I was probably at least a thousand yards from another person. I mean, I could barely see them off in the distance but they wouldn't have known if I'd gotten in trouble."

Additionally, Tommy had the tennis shoes, which greatly increased his chances of slipping a foot through the stirrup and being dragged. And then there was the cold, hard, rocky ground. There is a theory that if you throw yourself from a bucking horse, you may have some control over where your body lands. If the horse throws you, the horse controls where you land. Tommy decided to check out.

"Capîtan bucked right as I was trying to get off and he threw me probably twelve feet in the air," said Tommy. "And of course I'm like, horizontal. I'm up there flailing in the air and I came down and hit so hard I thought it knocked me out. It didn't, but it took me so long to get over the soreness, I mean I couldn't get out of bed the next day."

Amazingly, when Tommy fell the only thing he broke was his ego. And there was a little damage to his pride, as well.

"I wouldn't have actually told anybody what happened," said Tommy. "But my mom saw me hit the dirt. So when I rode up, she had a couple of words of encouragement like, 'I thought you were a big time bull-riding cowboy.'"

Tommy's parents, coming from a rodeo background, laughed about the incident.

"They're like, 'Way to go, big cowboy.' And I was like, 'No, you don't understand. We were at a dead run and he bucked hard.' They said, 'No, he just hopped a little bit and you fell off.' I'm like, 'No. He was bucking. Real hard.' And of course they're laughing because they'd seen this horse buck."

Three days later, Tommy was not only still full of aches and pains, he was literally still so sore he could hardly move.

"My dad was like, 'Yeah, you're going to be some kind of bull rider. That's just one time you hit the ground hard. Well, let me tell you son, there's only one way to exit a bull and that's: you hit the ground.'"

Tommy quickly realized that he wasn't going to be able to deal with the hard landing that comes with bull riding.

"If I had to do the ride all over again," said Tommy thoughtfully, "I'd probably try to ride Capîtan out, just because of the ribbing I took from my parents. I would have taken the chance and tried to stay on. If I had boots on. . .losing a stirrup right off the bat is a little disheartening."

Tommy later was told that shortly after the Steiners bought Capîtan they tried to return him. His previous owner had neglected to mention his penchant for bucking. He also wanted no part of having the horse back. A deal as they say, is a deal. Capîtan apparently was a very good horse, and extremely fast, but his riders never could tell when he'd start to buck. Capîtan ended up throwing so many people, in fact, that the Steiners ended up putting him in a rodeo just to see how he'd buck.

"I'm sitting there watching it all, because I want to see this horse buck like he bucked with me. It was basically payback, us putting him in the rodeo," said Tommy. "This bareback rider was getting on him and he's putting his hand in the rigging and I hear one cowboy going, 'What do you know about this horse,' and another's going, 'I don't know. It's somewhere from the Steiner Ranch,' and the first guy was going, 'Really?' and he was like, 'Yeah, he keeps bucking all of them off.'

"When the gate opened, I'm like all excited and ready for all this action, and Capîtan just kind of hopped out there. It was so funny. He just hopped out there with a flank strap on. I was like, 'Ooohhhh, Ooooohhh, that's not how he bucked with me.'"

The Steiners ended up selling Capîtan for obvious reasons.

Tommy thinks the horse is probably somewhere bucking people off right now.

"It really was because of that horse that I am not a bull rider," said Tommy. "There's no way. Capîtan really did save me from that. I mean, I never could have handled that day in and day out. Right after that I decided to start singing. I thought, if I'm not going to be a bull rider, I might as well do something I want to do and I want to sing.

"I think horses are just incredibly athletic creatures and for that I enjoy watching them and being around them," said Tommy. "Growing up, I didn't have a choice and now, I'm glad I didn't have a choice. I like to get away and go out and just ride, but I always end up getting roped into something that can be considered work. Today, we run a little over two thousand registered Black Brangus. Anyone who has even five cows can tell you, you never really finish. There's always something to do. There's always something messed up, there's a fence down, whatever. So two thousand head is a complete wreck. I try to stay as far away from the ranch as possible. That's why I'm glad this whole music thing has worked out so well for me," he laughed. "Cause' the family'll go, 'Hey, can't you come out and visit us?' and I show up and it's always like. . .branding day. 'Hey, glad you could make it. Grab a horse.'"

And you can bet that when Tommy swings his leg over the saddle, he'll leave the tennis shoes at home and have his feet tucked firmly into his boots.

www.tommyshanesteiner.com

Tommy Shane Steiner Fan Club
P.O. Box 120726
Nashville, TN 37212

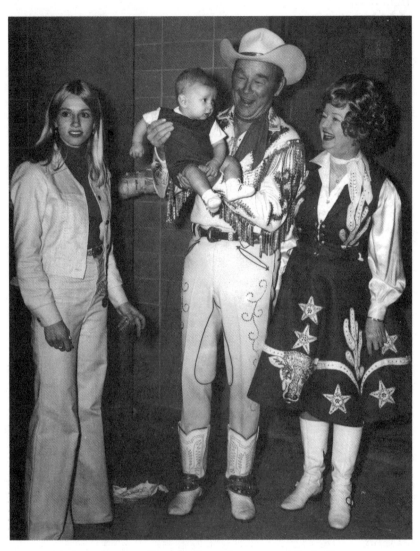

Joleen Steiner, Tommy, Roy Rogers and Dale Evans.

Joleen Steiner with young sons Sid and Tommy.

Sid and Tommy.

Mustang Sally

"Mustang Sally really holds their own when you put an instrument in their hands. They have a fun and enlightening show and their musicianship is superb. We had a great time performing with them."
Heath Wright, Ricochet

You've probably seen them at a fair or festival. They're the rocking all-girl band that has Music Row and fans worldwide all abuzz. And with good reason. From classic country to Southern rock, Mustang Sally is hot, hip and cool. This amazing girl group consists of six extremely talented ladies, a truckload of musical instruments, a veritable arsenal of great songs, and a stage show that rocks. It is a recipe that has been drawing crowds all over the world. They are, arguably, the best all-girl touring band anywhere.

Together a little over four years, Mustang Sally conducted a worldwide search for the best female vocalists and instrumentalists on the planet. Hailing from points as diverse as West Virginia and New Zealand, Mustang Sally offers edgy country music with a contemporary feel, and a fun, crazy stage show.

Their popularity has not gone unnoticed, and Mustang Sally has recently inked a recording contract with a major label. Meanwhile, the girls stay busy on the road bringing their music to fans everywhere from Seattle to Switzerland.

The band features Ryan Rygmyr on lead vocals, Debbie Johnson on bass and vocals, and Becky Priest on keyboards and vocals. Lynne Campbell handles lead guitar duties, while Lisa Romeo plays drums and adds harmony vocals. The wild one on fiddle, mandolin, sax and guitar is Renaé Truéx.

Mustang Sally's lead singer, Ryan Rygmyr, and bassist, Debbie Johnson, grew up a thousand miles apart, but their experiences around horses have been surprisingly similar.

"My parents had a lot of land and we had a lot of animals of all sorts running around, pets and farm animals both. It was a great place to grow up," said Ryan, who grew up in Duluth, Georgia.

Like many girls, Ryan was a horse lover from an early age. Her room was decorated with horse figurines and posters, and she'd pester everyone from the neighbors to the babysitter to talk horses with her. But the one thing that was missing from her young life was a real horse of her own.

"My mom realized that there was a lot of responsibility to having a horse and I think she didn't want me to have one until I was old enough to handle that responsibility," said Ryan. "And with a horse, you have to know a little bit about what you're doing. It's not like a dog, where you can just go play with it."

When Ryan was nine, she began taking riding lessons from a trainer who lived near them. Soon after, she was riding her very own horse.

"He was a little bay Shetland pony named Blaze," she said. "A man up the street owned him, and I guess everyone thought he'd be something safe for me to learn on, so we bought him. I remember being so excited when I got him because I had always, always, wanted a horse."

But like many little ponies, Blaze was not the nice, safe mount everyone thought him to be.

"Boy, he didn't cooperate at all," said Ryan. "He was a firecracker and really had a mind of his own. Blaze really was not the kind of a horse you wanted a nine-year-old to ride. I fell off of him a lot. A lot. But I always got up and got right back on and the good part about that was that he really helped me learn to ride—more so I think than if I had a horse that cooperated."

Ryan's trainer was into Thoroughbreds and hunter/jumpers. She began moving Ryan in that direction, and Ryan soon found herself making the rounds of the local horse shows.

"Oh, I'd do my hair up and stick it under the hunt cap and put on all the clothes and go out there and do my best," she said. Ryan first showed in walk/trot classes, but "the highest I ever placed with Blaze was third. And I think, considering how hard I had to work for that third, that that was pretty good. I am proud of that ribbon to this day."

But what Ryan much preferred to the controlled, precise movements of the show ring, was riding along a wooded trail, or out in an open field, the wind blowing through her hair and the drumming of hooves thumping in her ears.

"That was definitely my favorite thing—to go out on the trails and gallop through an open field," she said, the thought bringing exhilaration into her voice. "It is such a freeing experience to do that. You feel so alive. There is no other feeling in the world like that."

Ryan loved to ride, but she also loved the responsibility of caring for Blaze.

"I got up an hour early every morning before school to feed him. The hard part about all that was that we didn't have a barn," she explained. "We had Blaze in a field right by our house with some other horses. He was smaller than everyone else out there and I had to hold the bucket while he ate so the other horses wouldn't steal his food. So rain, sleet, snow, or hot weather, I was out there. But I never complained, because I liked doing it. My mom wanted me to learn responsibility and to understand how much work really was involved."

Ryan not only understood the responsibility, she thrived on it. So much so, that when Ryan was thirteen, her parents bought her an even-tempered chestnut Quarter Horse mare named China.

"I had pretty much outgrown Blaze by then," she said. "But the biggest change for me wasn't the size difference between Blaze and China—I had been riding several of my trainer's horses a lot by then—the big difference was that she was so much sweeter than Blaze, and a lot easier to work with. And that was a nice change."

Ryan recalls China as being four or five when she got her, but not terribly well-trained.

"She was willing, but she didn't really know what she was supposed to do. She wasn't as well-trained as I would have liked," she said. "But that also made me learn how to teach her the things I wanted her to know. So looking back, that was kind of a good thing."

Not too long after Ryan got China, a stallion somehow got into the field with her and impregnated the mare.

"We didn't realize it for a long time. We just had no idea, I mean, how would we? It wasn't something we were looking for, or expecting," she said. "And whoever had the stallion, or found the stallion in the field never said anything to us, or at least not to my parents, not to my knowledge anyway. I guess they were just hoping nothing had happened."

Something did happen and China ended up having a filly that Ryan named China Doll.

"She was so cute! I began working with her right away and that was tougher than I had thought it would be," said Ryan. "But I learned a lot through all that, patience mostly. And it was a lot of fun, too, to see the progress China Doll would make every time I worked with her. It was neat, because I could see a direct result from the effort I was putting in."

Prior to the birth of China Doll, Ryan had been showing China, mostly in lower level equitation and pleasure classes.

"I was slowly working my way up to hunter/jumper classes, but wasn't quite there, yet," she said. "I already could tell the difference in the stride of my Quarter Horse and in the Thoroughbreds I rode that my trainer had. The Thoroughbreds had a much longer stride, much better for jumping, than China. Of course, China was just 15.2, and the Thoroughbreds were 16.2, or 17-hands, and that just by itself will make a difference."

Ryan rode English—hunt seat—most of the time but "I would ride western sometimes, too. Western is a far more relaxed style of riding, very laid back. It's great for trail riding and you know I love trail riding, but back then I was training in English for horse shows so I spent far more time riding that style than I did western."

In addition to learning about hunter/jumpers and the horse show world, Ryan realizes that her trainer provided many other valuable lessons.

"She taught me about horses," said Ryan. "I spent a lot of time with my trainer. A lot. I was really into it. I was the only person she was training at the time so we really hung out together and did things, more than just regular lessons and stuff. I needed someone to show me about horses, how to groom them and what their body language meant. I needed someone to teach me what to look for when a horse was sick and how to help them learn and how to discipline them. Everything. Liking horses and knowing about horses are two different things, and she really helped me know about horses."

Even though Ryan loved horses deeply, by the time she was well into her teens, life, and music, began getting in the way of her commitment to China and her filly.

"It took me longer to get dressed in the mornings because by then I had to fix my hair just so before I went to school, and I was into all the usual teen activities—including singing—and the horses just kind of got lost in all that," said Ryan. "My parents drilled into me early on that if I wanted to have a horse that I had to take care of it. Somehow, my other activities became more important than the horses."

Ryan's family ended up selling China and China Doll to the man they bought Blaze from. The horses were close by and Ryan could see that they had a good home and were well cared for. But selling the horses is a decision she now regrets.

"I missed them, and just being around horses so much that my New Year's resolution for 2000—the big resolution year with the millennium and all—was to get back into horses," she said. "There has been this place inside me that has missed being around horses so much. I cannot wait until I am riding through a huge field again."

Ryan traded the open field and the drumming of hooves for a tour bus and the thumping of a bass guitar. But she now realizes it doesn't have to be an either/or situation. A new recording contract for the band, along with a heavy tour schedule limits her opportunities, but Ryan has several friends with horses and says she just likes to go hang at the barn.

"The thing I love most about horses is their personality," she said. "You just can't realize how much personality a horse has until you've had one of your own. They are all different. And once you know what to look for, they are great communicators, not like a dog or a cat, but in their own horse-like way. We can learn a lot if we can only try to see the world through their eyes."

Ryan realizes that horses have given her gifts far more important than the thrill of racing through a field of tall grass.

"Horses taught me to be dedicated to something I really loved and that has carried over into my music and into my life in general," she said. "I definitely learned early on that you can't just say, 'Hey, I want to do this,' and go get it. You have to work at it. You have to prioritize your life in order to make things happen. You have to have patience. You have to hang in there when things get tough and you can't quit just because you are cold, or because it's raining, or because you're tired. That's when you have to really kick in and work harder. Horses taught me that, and I learned very thoroughly that if you are not dedicated to the important things in your life, really dedicated, there's not much in life that will be dedicated to you."

Ryan and Debbie, along with the other four members of Mustang Sally mesh completely on-stage. That Ryan and Debbie's stories have some of the same elements should not be a surprise. As has Ryan, Debbie has loved horses all her life.

"I've been a horse fanatic I think since I was born," she said. "I think horses are so cool. When I was little, I didn't just read all the Margaret Henry books—I read every horse book I could get my hands on. And I drew horses constantly at school, at home, for art class. . ."

It wasn't until Debbie was in the sixth grade, after years of wanting and crying, that her parents bought her a horse.

"My horse was a beautiful Christmas present," said Debbie. "He was a registered Quarter Horse, sorrel, with a blaze down the center of his nose that was perfectly symmetrical and he had this little brown freckle right in the middle of it. There was no white anywhere else on him, no socks or anything. He was beautiful. He had a really nice chiseled head, and very nice conformation. His registered name was Joe Scoop."

Due to a mix up when she got the horse, Debbie was told his name was Barnaby. It wasn't until several months later when the registration papers came back, that they realized the mix-up, hence, around the barn, he became Barnaby Joe Scoop. A horse for her sister and one for her brother soon followed.

Debbie's family bought some land near their house to keep the horses on and went out to see them every day.

"My dad was very adept mechanically so he and I built a special feeder for them where we could put hay in the top. Eventually we made this automatic feeder so they would always get fed the same time every day, no matter what our schedule was," she said. "I used to get up an hour and a half early for school. My dad and I would go every single morning to feed and check on them.

"We never got into showing or rodeo," she continued, "but we had quite a bit of acreage so we rode there, and we took them to seminars, or to a friend's farm to ride."

Debbie fondly recalls the mutual love she and her horse had for each other.

"We'd go out there and you could always hear their hooves pounding on the ground as they came running up to see us. Barnaby would come up to me every time. Then he would just lay his whole head on my shoulder and inevitably slobber on me," she laughed. "It was green slobber—we called it the green goop—and it would get all over my shirts. Eventually all my shirts were stained on the sleeve where he would slobber all over me. It was funny. That was kind of his love kiss. He was a great horse, very beautiful, and so special to me."

Barnaby loved Debbie so much that Debbie's mother told her that the few times the rest of the family went to see the horses without her, that he didn't act the same.

"He was my baby. He was very special but in some ways he was quite a quirky horse," she said. "He used to carry around rocks in his mouth. I don't know what the deal was, but he had his own rock pile. He was so funny."

As with Ryan, Debbie feels that her horse taught her patience and responsibility. He also stretched her creative resources.

"Sometimes I'd get on him and he'd get ancy and jump around,"

she said. "Barnaby was real young, and real lively. I remember when
he acted like that I'd just sing to him. I'd get on and just trot him
around in the round corral where I'd practice my gaits, my leads, and
things like that. In the process, I'd sing to him and it usually made
him behave."

The horses are a part of Debbie's youth, and continue to be a big
part of her family history.

"Having horses really is the kind of thing that brings a family
together," she stated. "We can sit around the dinner table all these
years later and even though we don't have them anymore we can tell
funny horse stories and laugh for hours about them. We can just sit
around as a family, tell story after story, and just laugh so hard
because they are so funny. My brother's horse, I think, was a few
bricks shy of a load. He would put his head in the barn and stand
there and think he was in the shade. He was so funny."

When Debbie left Missouri for Nashville and college, she faced
the heartbreaking task of having to sell her beloved Barnaby.

"It was very upsetting when I had to get rid of him, but with me
not being there, it just wasn't practical to keep him," she said quiet-
ly. "Someday I will have horses again, I love them so much. I sure
loved my horse and riding, and my horse really, really loved me
back."

www.mustangsallyband.com

Mustang Sally Fan Club
1103 Bell Grimes Lane
Nashville, TN 37207

*Debbie's
Barnaby.*

Ryan and Blaze.

Roy Clark

"Clark and his crack troupe began a wondrous musical odyssey, dazzling the audience with his guitaristry, putting on a real live variety show, in the best sense of the phrase."
Country Music Live Magazine

Roy Clark is an extremely talented musician and vocalist who hosted the popular television show, Hee Haw, *for twenty-five years. He has been seen on many other shows as well, including a regular guest role on* The Beverly Hillbillies. *Roy went on to become the first country music artist to guest host* The Tonight Show *for Johnny Carson, and he has hosted many television specials, including* The Disney Anniversary Special, The Academy of Country Music Awards, *and three specials for England's BBC.*

Roy's achievements are breathtaking. He was the first national ambassador for UNICEF. He has received the Entertainer of the Year award from both the Academy of Country Music and the Country Music Association, and the Comedy Act of the Year from the Academy of Country Music. Roy was honored as Instrumentalist of the Year six times from the Music City News *awards; Picker of the Year from* Playboy *magazines reader's poll, Best Country Guitarist from* Guitar *magazine, and the list goes on and on.*

Roy's Grammy-winning virtuosity is showcased in his concerts but he is equally gifted with his generosity. It is impossible to mea-sure all the charitable causes he supports. The annual Roy Clark Celebrity Golf Tournament alone has raised millions of dollars for the Children's Medical Center in Tulsa and St. Jude Children's Research Hospital in Memphis.

Through the years, Roy has recorded a string of hits, including Honeymoon Feeling, *and* Thank God and Greyhound You're Gone, *but he is best associated with the stirring,* Yesterday When I Was Young *and his own twelve-string guitar version of* Malaguena.

Believing that music can bridge continents, Roy Clark has taken his message of goodwill to many countries around the world. But when Roy is home on his ranch near Tulsa, Oklahoma, his horses occupy much of his time.

From an early age, the highest highs and lowest lows in Roy Clark's life have been with horses.

"I guess ever since I was a kid there was something interesting to me about a cowboy movie and a horse," said Roy. "We never had riding horses around when I was young, but I used to ride mules and ride working horses back when I was six, seven-years-old. Five-years-old. I remember that I would always ride bareback."

When Roy was in his early twenties, he and a friend grabbed some horses and went riding.

"I think the horse I was on was a Morgan. This was in the early spring. This horse belonged to my friend and I know the horse had not been ridden since the previous fall so he was a little skittish, but not too bad," said Roy.

Roy's friend also had a German Shepherd, and as the two friends were riding, the dog started barking and nipping at the horses.

"Well, as long as my horse could see this dog, he was all right," Roy explained. "But the dog got under his back feet and my horse started rearing up. Looking back, if I had just given the horse his head, we'd have been all right. But when he reared up, you know, I got scared and started pulling back on the reins. The horse had a Mexican bit and if you are familiar with them you know when you pull back it can cut the roof of their mouth. But I kept pulling back and pulling back. This poor horse got up on his hind feet and started walking backwards and he hit a little up bank and I was pulling on that bit in his mouth, and really, it forced him over. I felt him fall. But by that time, I had slid off and was sitting on the ground. I had just turned to get out of the way when he just fell backwards across my leg."

Roy broke both bones in his leg, straight across between the knee and ankle, and didn't walk for eleven months. To this day, Roy says he never blamed the horse, realizing that it was just a freak accident that happened. But because Roy was not able to get right back up on the horse, because he'd had eleven months of rehabilitation, his sub-conscious, unbeknownst to him, had gone to work.

"I've often heard that if you fall off or if you get hurt on a horse, to get back on as quick as you can so you don't build up a fear," said Roy. "Well, I physically couldn't, you know, get back on a horse for some time."

Fellow recording artist Elton Britt, (who around the time of World War II had the first million selling country record, a song called *There's a Star Spangled Banner Waving Somewhere*) was a friend of Roy's.

"Elton was a real horseman and outdoorsman, and about three years after my little mishap I went up to his little farm and he had a yearling colt he wanted to show me," said Roy. "So Elton took me out to a little round pen to show me this horse, and I realized that this was the first time I had been around a horse since that mishap. It had been years. And as I stepped over into the pen, this horse took two steps towards me, just two ordinary walking steps. He just walked over like any horse would, being inquisitive, kind of slowly, and I broke out in the coldest sweat and started shaking. Just uncontrol-lable shaking, and I realized that a real fear of horses had been in me since the accident, but it had been dormant. Because I had not been around horses, there had been nothing to bring my fear to the sur-face. Somehow I climbed back through the pen, but I was shaking and sweating like all get out."

Rationally, Roy knew that the horse that had hurt him had not meant to. He even takes full blame for the fall.

"A horse really will do everything it can not to hurt you," he said.

"I mean, if you fall off in front of a horse, he'd do his best to step over you. I'd fallen many times before. I'd ridden a horse down a grade and lost my balance and slid off. I slid right under that horse's feet and he stepped right on over the top of me so I wouldn't get hurt."

After the incident with the colt in the round pen, Roy understood that he had to do something to get over his fear.

"I realized how ridiculous this fear was. I knew logically that it was just a freak accident that I, myself, out of my own fear and ignorance had caused," he said. But it took some time for the shaking to go away.

A year or so later, Roy had the opportunity to go riding.

"I was out in West Texas and a friend had some horses and invited me to go out and ride," said Roy. "So I went out and got on a horse and that was it. It was okay. I had thought a lot about horses and the fall over that year and had been able to conquer my fear. I felt a little uneasy that first time I climbed aboard, but it didn't last very long. I think that time we rode two or three days. I was really elated that I could ride that horse. It was probably four years from the time I fell until I got back on. That expression about getting right back on after a fall is true. I mean it is true to the hilt."

That ride brought Roy's love of horses to the surface and he decided that he actively wanted them in his life. Through the help of another friend, Roy claimed a Thoroughbred racehorse at a track in Maryland. Roy's wife, Barbara, soon became extremely interested in the sport.

"She wasn't into the racing part so much as the horse itself. She really got into pedigrees and blood strains, what horses really crossed well with other horses and that part of it," explained Roy. "She was so excited about it that I gave her a Thoroughbred mare for Christmas one year. That was about twenty-nine years ago because we just last year had to put this horse, Seductive Lady, down. She was thirty-two-years-old. She was a bay horse, a beautiful-headed horse. When we retired her from racing we made a brood mare out of her. We sent her to Florida and bred her to Boldnesian who was a son of Bold Ruler. Well, her first foal, Bolductive, turned out to win about $236,000 for us. That was our first one so we were a little spoiled. And very proud, too, that we had taken this horse that I had given her for Christmas and she really turned out to be such a super brood mare. Through the years, we bred Seductive Lady to top studs in Kentucky and to Boldnesian in Florida."

When Bolductive's racing career was over, the Clark's put him out to stud. One thing led to another and they built a brood mare facility on their ranch in Northeast Oklahoma. Roy turned around one day and realized he had sixty horses on the place.

"After that we started cutting down on quantity and paid more attention to quality," he laughed.

Roy says that out of all the horses he's been around, Seductive Lady, is the one closest to his heart.

"Her life with us was like a fairy tale story," he said. "I bought her for my wife for Christmas and she ran so good for us for a long time."

Seductive Lady eventually developed a bone chip in her knee, and the Clark's veterinarian and trainer advised them not to go through the expense of repairing the joint.

"Everyone advised us that she was not really that expensive of a horse," said Roy, "that it was going to be an expensive operation and they didn't advise us to go through all that expense with no guarantee."

But Seductive Lady was more than just a horse to Roy and Barbara Clark. She was a thoughtful gift from one caring partner to another, and she represented their first success on the racetrack. So they took the chance.

"After the operation, the surgeon came back and said, 'Well, we're glad you made this decision,'" said Roy. "They said the bone chip was about the size of the end of my thumb. It was a big bone chip, but it had done no damage. It had not torn any ligaments or anything. So we put her back on the farm and let her rest for about a year and brought her back to the track and racing and she won some races. She always ran good for us. She was a very dependable horse. You know, I really miss looking out in the pasture and seeing her there. It's just not quite the same without her."

For Roy Clark, horses are unlike any other animal.

"Every horse I have found has their own personality, their own aura," he said. "When you get to know them, there are no two horses alike. They may be similar but they all have their different traits.

"And there is nothing—even as thrilling as the racing part of it is—that I think can come close to helping a mare have a foal, help pull it out, clean it off, help it to stand and see it start nursing. It does not take long, and then they're out there in the paddock, running around, jumping up and down and really enjoying life. And then you're starting them in training, and taking them to the track, seeing your colors on their back and seeing that horse running in a race. And you have been there since the very beginning, you know, to help pull that horse out.

"Just being around the different horses, you never know what to expect. They all have different personalities and just to see that is a wonder in itself. So horses really take your mind off any other problem that you have when you are around them. You come in off the road, you've been out on a long tour, you go to the farm and start just walking around the horses, seeing how they are maturing. You just go into a different world and boy, that's a wonderful place."

www.roy-clark.com

Roy Clark International Fan Club
P.O. Box 148258
Nashville, TN 37214

Barbara and Roy Clark with Bolductive.

Roy with The Australian Kid, a champion
Appaloosa he owned for many years.

Toby Keith

"Keith owns a lethal tremolo and knows his way around a bal-lad. He may be a bit of a late bloomer, but Mr. Keith is ready for star-dom—now."
Billboard

Oklahoma native Toby Keith became interested in country music as a child, idolizing the musicians who played at his grandmother's supper club. He began playing guitar at age eight, but other pursuits beckoned as well. In high school, he worked as a rodeo hand for the rodeo company adjacent to his parent's farm and played high school football. But after graduation, Toby took a job in the oil fields. He never lost his love for music, though, and formed a band called Easy Money that played local honky-tonks on weekends. Music, however, remained on the sidelines while Toby did three years in the oil fields.

The oil industry hit a slump about the same time the United States Football League was forming. Toby tried out for the semi-pro Oklahoma City Drillers (a farm team for the Tulsa Outlaws) and made the cut. "I missed playing football so bad," Toby says. "I wished I'd kicked my butt in high school and gone on to play in col-lege." At 6-foot-4 and 235 pounds, Toby played defensive end for two years, and still found time to perform with his band. With the foot-ball league on shaky ground, Toby took stock of his life, and decided to draw from his strengths—singing and writing—and he attacked his musical career head-on. For seven years Toby and Easy Money worked the road, with Toby eventually landing a recording deal with Mercury Records. His self-titled 1993 debut disc scored three number one tunes and a top five hit including, Should've Been a Cowboy *and* A Little Less Talk and a Lot More Action.

In early 1999 Toby Keith signed with DreamWorks Records and became a true force in the industry when he unveiled How Do You Like Me Now?! *later that year. "There was zero attitude in country music," Toby said of the time. "Everything was so clean and predictable and middle-of-the-road, they rode that horse into the ground. But there's so much traffic in the middle of the road that you don't get very far. I stayed in the ditches off to the side. I just did my own thing. I am what I am. I wasn't afraid of attitude."*

Attitude worked. Toby was named Country Music Television's Male Video Artist of the Year and How Do You Like Me Now?! *was Country Music Television's Video of the Year in 2000. In 2001, Toby was named the Academy of Country Music's top male vocalist.*

His most recent disc, Pull My Chain, *furthers Toby's status. From* I'm Just Talkin' About Tonight *to* I Wanna Talk About Me, *Toby rubs against the grain of the safe and ordinary. "I worked hard to get here, but the real work has just started," he said. "It's like horses, you have to run them or they'll never separate themselves from the pack." Toby has surely, finally, done that himself.*

Toby has recently expanded his career to include acting, playing himself in the CBS television movie reunion of The Dukes of Hazzard *and starring in a series of commercials for the 10-10-220 long-distance telephone service.*

Now Toby has realized another lifelong ambition with the establishment of Dream Walkin Farms, a Thoroughbred breeding and training facility near Oklahoma City. He says his interest in horses will take him far beyond his touring days and gives him a thrill that he only elsewhere finds on stage.

Toby Keith loves a rush. Whether it is the thunderous applause of thousands of screaming fans, or the thunderous beat of a thousand pounds of Thoroughbred horseflesh crossing the finish line, Toby's adrenaline starts pumping.

"In my business, in entertainment, there is a little window of time that you have at the top. Then, when you're done, everyone heads out to the golf course," said Toby. "Golf doesn't do it for me and apparently it didn't do it for Michael Jordan either because he came back, and then he came back again. Golf wasn't providing the rush he found on the basketball court."

What does do it for Toby is horse racing.

"There is nothing like that rush, that thrill of hearing the announcer call your horse's name first as he crosses the finish line," Toby said, warming to the subject. "And it's not just the racing part for me. Researching the pedigrees is exhilarating. I love everything from finding the right mares, and choosing the right stallions for the mares, to the kick of naming the foals, and weaning them, and watching them turn into yearlings and shipping them off to the track, and starting the two-year-olds and finally seeing them come flying down the track and crossing the finish line. The whole process is such a high."

When Toby was a kid, his family bought a black Appaloosa mare. She had the traditional Appaloosa coat pattern of a white "blanket" over the hips with dark spots in the blanket. Sugar was in foal and the resulting baby, Chukka, was his first experience in raising a foal.

"Sugar was a great little horse and I spent a lot of time on her back," he said.

But Sugar did not have any special training. She was a nice safe mount for a kid, but she wasn't a show or a competition horse and she wasn't fine-tuned in any way. As he got older, Toby spent some time as a rodeo hand. He rode a lot of ranch horses, and did time riding his share of rodeo stock.

"For a long time I thought all horses were created equal," he said. "I'd ridden Sugar and some other horses that were around and I'd ridden a lot of rough stock. I remember very clearly the first time I climbed on a competition horse. It was a barrel horse that had a lot of speed and would respond with just a touch of your leg. He was so fast that he could mow anything else around at five hundred yards. I thought how amazing it was that a horse could be so quick and fast and smooth and sensitive. I'd had no idea."

The experience opened Toby's eyes to the many different possibilities that horses could present to him, both in business and as a recreational pursuit.

"I didn't realize it at the time, but I think the seed for what I am doing now with horses was planted that day," he said.

Today, Toby splits his herd of Thoroughbred brood mares and race horses on two Oklahoma ranches.

"We have the mares and the babies at the ranch at home," he said, "and then we have another ranch forty miles away where we have a weanling paddock, and a yearling paddock, and a training track, and stalls. We have everything there that you need to start the horses and get them used to racing."

Thoroughbreds from Toby's Dream Walkin Farms can be found running at any number of tracks across the country including Fairgrounds, Arlington, Oaklawn, and Churchill Downs. He uses several trainers and often has horses running both in the Mid-West and on the West Coast.

One of the things, Toby said, that he likes best about his involvement with horses, is that just like his music career, it is a year round operation.

"It's just like touring," he said. "I am comfortable in knowing that there is always something going on, some thrill to be had. When May comes around all the babies have been born and what a great thing that is. Just watching some of the younger horses working out, knowing the promise that they have, and down the road the excitement of seeing that fulfilled, that really gets me going."

There is a great deal of knowledge and horse sense that needs to be absorbed before anyone can be a successful breeder or owner, and Toby and his sister spend a great deal of time poring over pedigree books and charts, analyzing race results and workout times, and choosing names for the foals.

"My sister and I get a real kick out of going back into our past, back into our childhood and naming the babies something that means something only to us. It's our little inside joke that the rest of the world knows nothing about. We especially try to do this if it is a horse we think we are going to keep and race ourselves, we try to tag it with a name that has some significance to us," he said.

For example?

"Well," he said with a chuckle, "When we were kids—I was about five or six and my sister was four or five—my parents were just getting started in life and we lived in this old apartment building called Reagan Court. We named this one horse Reagan Court and we just love hearing the announcer calling the name Reagan Court in a race. And only my sister and I know this fancy Thoroughbred horse is named for an old run down apartment building."

Mixing the names of a foal's sire and dam, or putting a clever twist on the mix is one way to name a horse. Toby and his sister tagged another horse, the offspring of Bugs Rabbit and Gilded Time, as Golden Hare.

Toby says that even though he enjoys it, life on the road prevents him from doing much riding much these days. But he is quick to add that it is important to him to be sure that there are always a couple of horses at the ranch for his kids to ride.

"My own love is in planning the birth of these horses, and in the training, and all the way through the racing, and until they themselves are producing new babies," he said. "But we do have two horses now that my kids ride, a dark bay mare that is a competition horse and an old palomino that the neighbors have."

As Toby heads to yet another performance date, as he completes another interview, and writes one more song that will hit the charts several years down the road, you know that somewhere in there he's going to find time to check out the pedigree of the latest Derby winner and touch base with his ranch manager.

"The best thing about this is I know that horse racing is something that will take me well beyond my time on the road," said Toby. "In the music business, I have a little longer window of opportunity than a professional athlete does, but I know my time as an entertainer is here and now and I'll ride it as long as I can. And I'll enjoy the ride tremendously.

"But when I decide it's over, I will have something that excites me equally as much as singing and recording and the road. And it's the horses. If I retired tomorrow, I'd be happy and I don't know how many other artists could say that. It's hard to replace that high that you get from the fans, that total exhilarating thrill you get from being on stage, but I've found it. The only thing that I like equally as much as I do performing, is horses. I'll always have them, they'll always be it for me. Horses are my future."

www.tobykeith.com

Toby Keith Fan Club
P.O. Box 8739
Rockford, IL 61126

Wild Horses

"I heard one new artist this year that impressed me. One. It was Wild Horses."
J.D. Haas Enterprises and Radio Trip Promotions

They call their concerts the frontier-free-for-all—a visual and sensory explosion of sound and movement. Some say it's the equivalent of a heart thumping, seat shaking, sensurround action movie.

Fronted by Angela Rae, a sexy female lead who sets the other Horses, as well as the audience, on fire, Wild Horses ignites their concerts. Together for close to a decade, this five-piece band has created one of the most exciting concert experiences ever encountered. Yes, they are all over the stage. Yes, Wild Horses are just as much fun to watch as to listen to. But they have not forgotten the sound or the songs. Their soaring harmonies and their thought-provoking lyrics have fans thinking about the music long after Wild Horses have left town. And when Wild Horses are there, the fans dance. On tables. On chairs. Sometimes even on stage. Everyone gets caught in the spirit when Wild Horses are in the house.

For the past few years, Wild Horses have toured roughly two hundred dates a year, revving their music across the country. From the National Finals Rodeo and Houston Livestock Show and Rodeo to corporate parties, state fair grounds, and dance clubs nationwide,

Wild Horses are gaining fans everywhere. Currently signed to Epic Records, Wild Horses are setting the stage for an explosive career. Watch for them. They'll see you on the frontier.

In addition to being one of the hardest working bands to ever come out of the Nashville machine, all five members of Wild Horses are horse people. That means they are good people. They call their fans their friends, and when you meet them, you'll know why. You feel as if you've known them forever.

Michael Blake Mahler plays an assortment of instruments, including mandolin, and helps the group with harmony vocals. Born in Temple, Texas and raised in nearby Heidenheimer in a farm/ranch environment, Michael remembers riding in a 4th of July parade with his Dad when he was five.

"In Belton, Texas, everyone who wants to, rides their horses at the end of the parade, so pretty much there are miles and miles of horses coming," he said. "I remember in the parade I was riding in front of my dad on a big Quarter Horse we had named King. I had my own horse then, Ringo, a little paint. He was cool. I remember I could ride then, but not well enough for a parade. That's how long I've been around horses. All my life."

Drummer Ralph (Thundersticks) McCauley was born in Needville, Texas and raised on a 10,000 acre ranch.

"My first horse was a Quarter Horse called Traveler. He was really my dad's horse, but he was very calm and good for kids. I guess you could say I learned to ride because I got tired of falling off," joked Ralph. "As I was growing up, I was taught that horses are very special, very spiritual. For me, they're family members."

Like Michael, Joe Lee Koenig grew up in Heidenheimer, Texas. He plays rhythm guitar and sings harmony with Wild Horses.

"When I was very young, I learned to ride on a little black Shetland pony named Cricket," he said. "In fact, I used to ride with Michael and some other kids." Cricket was owned by a childhood friend (Joe's family did not have horses) and he remembers riding regularly when he was in grade school.

The only non-Texan in the group, bassist Steve Kellough was

born in Evansville, Indiana. The son of a minister, Steve started singing gospel music at age five and added bass guitar after his mother taught him to play. His family also had ponies when he was young."

I remember my dad coming home from church all dressed up nice in his Sunday suit and catching the ponies for us so we could ride," said Steve. "We had some great times with those ponies."

But it is lead singer Angela Rae's story that typifies Wild Horses as a band. Angela was also born in Temple, Texas. While in her teens she became involved in musical theater and performed in Joseph and the Amazing Technicolor Dreamcoat. Her first horse was a pony she received when she was about eight.

"My dad grew up in Virginia and he had a horse that he'd always tell us about that he said was the best horse in the world," said Angela. "He would lay on that horse's back and he would fall asleep on this horse. When he'd wake up this horse would automatically take him back home. It was a horse they could take up in the mountains and when I was young I always thought that was cool.

"I guess I was about eight, and my brother Stan was about nine," she said, "when my daddy decided to get us each a horse. He had such a great experience with the horse he had when he was young, he wanted that for us as well. We started with two Shetland ponies at first, Blazin and Scooter. Scooter was a light brown, tan almost, with a very light mane and tail. Blazin was a bay, brown with a black mane and tail. We had them for about three months and were getting used to riding when my dad decided he was going to get a bigger horse for my brother. He ended up getting my brother a real nice Quarter Horse named Dolly, but she was pretty spunky. She usually minded, but if she got the urge to take off and run, she would."

One hot Texas summer day Angela and Stan decided to go riding. Stan took Dolly and Angela rode Scooter. They seldom put saddles on their horses, instead preferring to ride bareback in an open field next to their house. The land around the property where Angela's family lived, the area where they rode their horses, was not fenced and there was a fairly busy paved farm road in front of the house.

Angela remembers her father as being very strict. He made sure his children knew they had to mind him and why, and they respected him a great deal.

"Because of the road and the open field, my dad said, 'Whatever you do, you do not let these horses go. Don't ever let go of the bridle, always hang on to them. Don't ever let the horses go, because we don't want them to run away or cause an accident on this road.' Angela said it was typical of her dad to be thinking of others. He didn't want to cause anyone else any inconvenience if his children were neglectful and let the horses roam free.

"I always tried very hard to please my dad, so I said, 'Okay, I won't ever let go. I'll make sure I'll hold on.'"

Angela and Stan, both riding bareback, were having a nice, pleasant ride well out into the flat, open field adjacent to their house. Angela was having fun, but when she rode there was always a tiny seed of doubt in the back of her mind. She wasn't all that sure of her abilities.

"You know how Shetland ponies are," she said. "When they start trotting it's always these real short, choppy, up and down, bouncy steps. So I told my brother, 'Whatever you do, don't start going fast.' We'd only been riding a few months and I thought that without a saddle, I may not be able to hang on very well."

At the far end of the field, nearly a quarter mile away from their house, the two turned to head back. At the distant sight of the barn, Dolly, who was apparently a little barn sour, quickly bolted across the field.

"My brother tried, but he couldn't really stop her, you know, he was just nine," said Angela.

Of course the natural consequence of one horse bolting across the field, is for both horses to bolt across the field. But maybe Angela was a little better rider than she thought, or very likely the pony was not as strong as Dolly, or it could be that Angela had her daddy's words fresh in her mind. Because instead of a dead run, Angela held little Scooter's pursuit of Dolly to a brisk trot.

"That's what messed me up," laughed Angela, "when he started trotting, because it was so rough. I started sliding to the side and I started squeezing my legs, trying to hang on."

Before too long, gravity prevailed and Angela slid off. When she fell, all she could think about were the words her dad had so effectively drilled into her mind. 'Do not let go of the horse. Do not let go.' So Angela didn't let go. She hung on with all she had.

"Here I am hanging on to the bridle and he drug me not the full quarter of a mile, but I think maybe it was two hundred yards," she said. "He drug me all the way to the house. You see Dolly just ran and kept running until she got to the house. So Scooter was just dragging me along with him the whole way."

As it was hot and in the summer, little Angela was dressed in shorts and a thin summer top. Her mother watched the entire incident from the house, and from all accounts was scared to death.

"We went through weeds and stickers and briars," said Angela. "By the time we got to the house, my legs were bleeding, and I had cuts and scratches on my side. It was a miracle I didn't get stepped on. The whole time we were headed back to the house, I was bumping along off to the side of Scooter, hanging on to the reins for all I was worth. It was just me and Scooter and the weeds and dirt and rocks. I had my eyes closed and I remember just being whipped around. The only thing I could think about when we got back to the house was that I was so proud of myself that I didn't let go. Of course my dad felt horrible. He said, 'You know Angela, I didn't want you to let go of the horse, but you could have been really hurt, really hurt badly. I'd rather you let go then get hurt.'"

Angela's reluctance to let go, her and her willingness to take the risk of being hurt is really a summery of the career of all members of Wild Horses. For more than ten years the group has been bumped and whipped around the music business. Several record deals, some with major labels, have come and gone without ever having musical product released. Their current recording contract with Epic Records is the result of sheer determination and blind faith, faith such as Angela showed in hanging on to the reins. Her daddy said it was right and she trusted and respected her daddy. So she was going to hang on.

"We, all of us, have never let go of the dream of making it in the music business," said Angela. "I wasn't going to let go of that horse and I'm not letting go of this career. I'm just too hard headed to quit."

After being dragged, Angela learned to wear jeans when she

rode, and she learned that she has the determination and the reserves deep within to accomplish seemingly impossible things. She also learned that to succeed at your dreams, you have to practice until you are very, very good. So she made a conscious effort to learn to become a better rider, and she, along with the rest of Wild Horses, are among the best prepared when it comes to every aspect of their career. She also learned to trust her instincts. If something doesn't feel right, don't do it. Angela didn't feel she had the capability to stop Scooter if he began a faster pace, and she didn't. So Angela learned that sometimes you have to back up a step before you can go forward. Before you can ride out in the open field, you have to be a good enough rider to handle the horse. She also learned patience. Maybe you can't ride in the field now, but if you sit back, take your time, practice and improve your skills, then you can ride anywhere you want.

Angela and the rest of the Horses have been very patient in their career. They are always improving their skills and carefully planning the next step, with the ultimate goal of a stellar career in sight. And for Angela, a little Shetland pony named Scooter helped make it all happen.

www.wildhorsesband.com

Wild Horses Fan Club
P.O. Box 8924
Bossier City, LA 71113

Above: Angela Rae with Dazzle, owned by Joni Werthan, Franklin, Tennessee.

Right: Ralph McCauley, in 1965.

John Berry

"If there is a more commanding vocalist in country music than [John] Berry, we have yet to hear from him."
Ed Morris, *Nashville Scene*

Like many of today's top country artists, John Berry grew up at a time when popular music embraced a wide array of styles. In the same way that Bob Wills incorporated jazz to produce Western Swing, and Waylon Jennings pulled rock-and-roll into his "outlaw" country, John adapted bits and pieces from his various musical predecessors into his own unique style. James Taylor, Willie Nelson, Cat Stevens, Neil Young, Vern Gosdin, the Charlie Daniels Band, the Doobie Brothers, and the Philadelphia sound of groups like the Chi-Lites and the Stylistics all contributed to John's eclectic mix. That creative conglomeration of styles, backed by John's incredible, soaring tenor, struck a huge chord with fans and professionals alike. A Georgia native, John released six albums on his own before arriving in Nashville in 1992 and being added to the Capitol Nashville roster.

Soon after his first Capitol release, a crisis struck. John should have been excited over his exploding career and the recent birth of a son. Instead, he was tired and in severe pain. A visit to the doctor revealed that John had a cyst on his brain. He underwent successful emergency surgery, and quickly went back to work.

With hits such as Your Love Amazes Me, Standing on the Edge of Goodbye, *and* If I Had Any Pride Left at All, *it is difficult to find an artist more passionate about their music, or more devoted to bringing music to an audience than John Berry. But John says that he learned the patience he needed to balance his career with other equally important areas of his life from an odd friendship with a cranky old mare.*

John Berry has had a life-long admiration of horses. He had always wanted a horse, and was thrilled when he purchased his first horse in 1986.

"He was a Tennessee Walker and he was really something," said John. "He was a sorrel roan, a beautiful horse. His name was Buttons and I just absolutely loved him."

John said he has always been fascinated with horses, and before buying Buttons grabbed the chance to ride with friends whenever the opportunity arose.

"I was living in Athens [Georgia] in '85 and I had gone out riding with someone and thought, 'You know what? I'm single. I'm making a real living here. I can afford to do this.' So I found this horse at a place not far from where I was living, and I was able to board him there, too."

John loved everything about being a horse owner so much that he ended up going out to the barn on Saturdays and Sundays, working there as a trade out for boarding.

"I got to feed the horses and clean the stalls," he said. "I can't tell you how much I enjoyed all that. It was just so nice. It was a total blast."

Today, John, his wife, Robyn, and their three children, Taylor Marie, 12, Shaun, 8, and Caelan James, 7, have four horses. Two are kept on their property, and two on a neighboring farm that backs up to their property.

"All my kids like riding, but my son Caelan is obsessed with horses," said John in his soft-spoken voice. "He lives and breathes horses—it's all he talks about."

Caelan apparently loves all horses, but he is totally obsessed with one horse in particular, an unusual horse that used to belong to his father.

"Poca is an older black Quarter Horse mare," said John. "She is very black during the summer. But during the wintertime she's almost mule looking—she gets a lot of brown around her nose.

"I hate to say this, but Poca is not a very nice horse. As a matter of fact, she has one of the nastiest attitudes I've ever been around. But the funny thing is, Caelan loves her to death. He doesn't want to ride any other horse. And I can understand that, because I have a great deal of affection for Poca, also."

Poca came into John's hands in an almost comical manner. The owner of a club John was performing at won the mare in a poker game. The opponent owed the club owner two hundred and fifty dollars and didn't have it, so they settled on the horse instead. The only problem was that Poca's new owner suddenly needed a place to keep her. John had a 140-acre farm at the time and quickly agreed to care for her.

"We loved this horse and took care of her and rode her for something like four, five years, and the guy who won her in the poker game had never even come to see her in all that time," said John in amazement. "So finally Robyn, my wife, called him up and said, 'You know you really need to send us the papers on this horse,' and he did."

John has now had Poca for more than twelve years and says that one of the interesting things about her is that she's been brushed and fed and loved every day for so many years and she's still just as mean as a hornet.

"You have to watch yourself around her. You can't let people who don't know about horses get around her because she'll kick them or bite them or something," he said. "She's never kicked me. She's attempted to, but I'm just very aware when I'm around her. I keep an eye on her all the time. It's obvious that she's come from some serious abuse down the line because she'll turn around and nip at me and if I am startled and turn around real quick, it's like oh, boy. Poca gets this total look of terror on her face, like she thinks she's fixing to just get beat to a pulp. And it just breaks my heart."

Even though Poca is ornery. Even though she is a handful. Even though she goes out of her way to be mean and hateful, and would as soon kick most people as look at them, Poca is still the ride of choice for both John and Caelan.

"Another horse that we have, Rebel, is really a perfect child's horse. She's a big roan Quarter Horse mare. She's almost 17-hands and just a beautiful, beautiful animal, just a pleasure to ride. She'll do anything you ask, and she wouldn't hurt anybody," said John. "The first day we had her we had kids riding her around the back yard with just a halter and a lead rope. You couldn't do that with Poca in a million years.

"But there's just something about Poca that I really like. Maybe it's because I've had her for so many years, or maybe it is our history together. I don't know. But I always ride her. Robyn says, 'That horse hates everybody in the world but you.' And she says that as Poca's trying to kick me. But when I ride her, she will do whatever I ask. I don't have to force her, I don't carry a crop or any of that kind of stuff. I'm always gentle on the bit with her and she always does what I want her to do. And I can't say she's that way with anybody else, except Caelan."

John performs a number of live shows each year which keeps him on the road and away from the barn, but if the weather cooperates and John is home, he and the boys make a habit of riding almost every day.

"Of course, I walk. Shaun and Caelan ride. They're pretty young yet," said John. "And we're all still pretty cautious around Poca. She throws a fit when I saddle her up but the minute I put the bit on there's this physical change that takes place. All of a sudden she becomes very controllable. She actually fools you into thinking that you can actually go ride her at that point. It's just one of those things. I would anticipate that she'll never change from that. That's just the way she is. She's pushing twenty and it's such a shame, because this little fellow just loves her more than anything in the world. Everyone should be lucky enough to have someone love them as much as Caelan loves Poca. I don't know if Caelan will ever be to the age that he can ride her by himself. I don't know if she'll ever live that long. We'll see."

Poca is not a big mare, standing about 15.2, but she takes her aggressive attitude to the pasture as well, serving as the dominant lead mare in the Berry's small herd.

"She doesn't take anything from anybody. When we put her in with new horses, she just raises cain," said John. "I sometimes wonder what experiences she has had to make her that way and hope that some of the kindness we've shown her has helped her enjoy life a little more, helped her to realize that all people aren't bad."

It is important to John that he give to Poca and help her overcome her fear, because in her own way Poca has given a lot to John and to his family.

"Patience," he said emphatically. "That is one of the things we stress with the kids around Poca, and around all the horses—that you have to be very calm and be very patient. You don't raise your voice. You don't raise a ruckus. You don't slam the gates. It is a very calming thing for me to be around Poca, even though she is high spirited and she can be temperamental. Knowing that she is that way, it gives an opportunity to create a very calm environment around her. And that calmness, that patience that I've had to develop, transcends to other areas of my life. There is a peace that I have developed partly because of my interaction with Poca, and that peace has become a very important part of just about everything that I do."

John says he enjoys the activities around his horses almost as much as being around the horses themselves, and he is encouraging his kids, and others, to learn as much as they can about the entire spectrum horses have to offer.

"There's a place near us that we're putting our boys in this spring," said John "It's an after school program with an emphasis on horses. There are places around where you just go one or two days a week and you clean stalls and brush horses, and you just get into that great vibe of being around them. Just being around horses, enjoying their companionship, to me is just as important as the riding part, if not more so. I would strongly advise someone to do that before they buy one, because it gives you a chance to figure out what kind of horse you like, what kind of ride you want to go on. Do you want to do a hunter jumper thing and ride in a ring or do you want to trail ride? Being in that kind of a learning environment gives you a lot of different options to experience before buying a horse, and keeps you from wasting money on the kind of horse you won't enjoy riding."

And Poca?

"She'll have a home with us until she dies," said John. "She's like the black sheep you can find in every family. You don't always like them, you don't always agree with them or what they do or with their actions, but you always love them."

www.johnberry.net
www.johnberryradio.com

John Berry's Fan Club
P.O. Box 121162
Nashville, TN 37212

George Jones

*"Over four decades have passed since fans first heard the raw, emo-
tional, heart-on-his-sleeve delivery that is instantly identifiable as
George Jones. . .Jones knows heartache songs every bit as well as he
knows drinking songs. He can put a positive spin on a history of
pain."*
countrystars.com

*George Glenn Jones was born in Saratoga, Texas. As a kid, he
sang for tips on the streets of nearby Beaumont. By age twenty-four,
he had been married twice, served in the Marines and was a veteran
of the Texas honky tonk circuit.*

*He first hit the charts in the 1950s and is one of only a handful
of artists who can count number-one records in every decade since.
George is regarded by many as the world's leading honky-tonk
singer, and has the life and the career to prove it. He was voted Male
Vocalist of the Year for the Country Music Association in 1962 and
again in 1963.*

The hits kept coming. His video for Who's Gonna Fill Their
Shoes *won the Country Music Association's Video of the Year in
1986. In 1992 the Country Music Association recognized Jones's
monumental career by inducting him into the Country Music Hall of
Fame. A few years later, in 1996, he released his autobiography,* I

Lived To Tell It All, *which made the* New York Times *bestseller list and was followed by a new album of the same title.*

In 1999, George celebrated the fortieth anniversary of his first number-one record, White Lightning. *It was also the year that he won his second Grammy for Best Male Country Vocalist, this one for his performance on the single,* Choices. *His only previous Grammy was in 1981 for his performance of* He Stopped Loving Her Today. *That song earned him Single of the Year honors from the Country Music Association in 1980 and again in 1981, along with virtually every other award available. The song remained number-one for eighteen weeks.*

His well-publicized marriage to Tammy Wynette was stormy but in the recording studio they were the perfect duet partners, hitting number-one with We're Gonna Hold On *and, coinciding with their 1976 divorce,* Golden Ring *and* Near You.

Choices *marked George's 164th charted record. In fact, George Jones has had more charted singles than any other artist in any format in the history of popular music. An incredible record for an incredible career.*

Over the years George has realized that it's the simple things in life that bring him joy and relaxation. And throughout his life, George has found horses to be one of the simple pleasures that life brings.

George Jones grew up in a very rural community in East Texas. If people in George's neck of the woods were lucky enough to have a horse, it was definitely a horse that earned its keep. More likely, instead of a horse, they'd have a work-worn mule. In the thirties and early forties, when George was a small boy, he often spent summers at the home of a sister and brother-in-law. They kept a mule and one summer day, with grasshoppers threatening to take over the cotton planted in the fields, George learned first hand just how not to spook a mule.

"We had a big, hand-made wooden sled with a railing around it that we hooked to this mule," said George. "I was supposed to hang on to this rail and drive this mule up and down the rows of cotton while Dub [George's brother-in-law] poured a mixture of bran and arsenic and syrup by hand over the cotton."

The mix was tasty to grasshoppers, but also lethal. At some point, George stopped the mule as he and Dub happily surveyed the growing number of dead insects. But there was more work to be done, so there was not a lot of time for reflection.

"I had just hollered at the mule to get going," George recalled, "when this dog cornered a skunk not too far from us."

But at the time, George and Dub didn't know it was a skunk, thinking instead that it might be one of the many varieties of poisonous snakes found in the area. They cautiously left the mule, and went to investigate.

"When we realized it was a skunk, we both lit out of there as fast as we could go," said George. "I was running and yelling toward the mule and mules aren't dumb. He knew something was up."

The mule apparently thought that if George was running and yelling, he should too. He promptly took off across the rows of cotton, flinging the tub of Dub's insecticide every which way and running through a barbed wire fence.

"The mule just took the fence and a gate clean out," said George. "I was all upset—the mule was bleeding, the fence and gate were ruined, the sled was a pile of broken pieces of wood, and I was sure Dub was going to whup me good."

Instead, Dub gave George a hug and together they spread ointment on the mule's cuts.

"You'd have thought that after that Dub wouldn't have trusted me to drive that mule. But he did," said George.

The next day George, Dub, and the mule were all back out in the field with more of Dub's homemade insect brew and at least part of the cotton crop was saved. The incident taught George a little bit about mules and a lot about people.

"That next day, I wasn't going to let go of that mule for anything," said George. "I didn't even let go when my sister came out to bring us lunch. I just ate with one hand holding on to those reins. And I had definitely learned not to run and scream and yell so's he'd take off."

George also learned that kindness and trust, and maybe even a second chance, go a lot further with a person than harsh words and a whipping.

When he was a little older, George would occasionally skip school and sneak off into the woods. Sometimes one of his many relatives would happen by on a mule and George would hop on behind, enjoying the ride, and the few hours of freedom. Since then, George's experiences with horses, even the long-eared variety, have been far more positive and constructive in nature.

"There's something about being around a horse that is relaxing to me," George said. "I have always found that to be true, but even more so now than before."

George has had many well-publicized ups and downs in his life and his career, but during a high point, around 1966, George bought a few acres in Texas and began stocking it with Appaloosas, Quarter Horses and some Black Angus cattle. He also built a house, a guesthouse, several livestock barns, a riding ring, and circled it all with beautiful post and rail fencing. There, George built up quite a herd of well-bred horses.

"I have always liked horses, Quarter Horses especially," said George. "And I love horse racing. There's nothing quite like seeing horses running toward the finish line."

During that time, George became so involved in his horses and in racing, that he was honored with an annual Quarter Horse race bearing his name at New Mexico's prestigious Ruidoso Downs racetrack.

Through the years, whenever George had a solid spell in his life and career, he'd always find a way to keep a horse or two. By the early 1990s he had established his Country Gold Farms just south of Nashville. He began breeding and raising the working variety of Quarter Horses, horses that instinctively knew how to cut cattle from a herd, and horses that had the speed and athletic ability to perform the hard sliding stop necessary to a good rope horse.

Along about 1996, one of George's daughters saw a miniature horse at a horse sale and came home very enthusiastic about the tiny animals. Before too long, George's Country Gold Farms had close to twenty of the miniatures.

"These horses are about the size of a real big dog, but they still eat like a horse," laughed George. "For a while we had a trainer and got into showing them and I enjoyed that very much. It was something my wife, Nancy, and I could do together that we both enjoyed that was away from the music business."

The miniature horses also provided some important one-on-one time for George and his grandchildren.

"We had a little buggy—a little carriage—that we'd hook one of them up to and we'd load up one of the grandkids and ride around. They loved it," he said.

George sold the miniatures in the late 1990s and, although the number varies from time to time, currently has just three horses: two Quarter Horses, and a big Clydesdale named Erin that someone gave him as a gift.

With George's busy touring schedule, someone needs to stay home and feed the animals. Since the first day of 1993, that job has fallen to Woody Woodruff. Woody takes care of all the cattle and horses, along with everything in between that goes along with their care.

"George just likes to get out here and look at the horses, lean on the fence and take it all in," said Woody. "Horses are therapeutic that way. When we've got them, he likes to watch the babies, too. They always bring a smile to his face."

The two Quarter Horses are mares, and while not currently nursing foals, they will be bred to cutting horses this year. One, a sorrel named Jolene, is in training for cutting, the other, a dun named Fancy, is more of a rope horse.

And while you probably won't see George Jones on the back of a cutting horse or roping cows any time soon, it doesn't mean that he doesn't get his own sense of satisfaction out of loving his horses from the ground. Indeed, George says he gets immense enjoyment out of watching his horses graze in the pasture.

"I find the horses very relaxing," he said, "and totally unlike the entertainment business with all the lies and politics on the business side. My fans have been very good to me and I've had a great career. I've been singing professionally for more than fifty years. I sing from my heart, I love country music and I love the people that respond to it. But sometimes I like to step back from that. I like walking around the fields and watching the sun set. I don't have nearly the time that I'd like to spend with the horses, but it brings something extra, and very nice, to my day to see them out there."

www.georgejones.com

George Jones Fan Club
296 Wine Branch Rd.
Murphy, NC 28906

George and a young Quarter Horse named Country.

Brooks & Dunn

"There are a few acts in Nashville that have successfully bridged the gap between the old and the new over the years, and among them is the talented duo of Kix Brooks and Ronnie Dunn, more commonly known as Brooks & Dunn. They are two of the most talented song-writers and musicians in the country music business. . .They've developed a knack for creating music that is appealing to the younger listeners, yet still definitely country."

Mitch Worthington, yourmvp.com

Brooks & Dunn have sold twenty-four million albums, had twenty-one of their songs hit number-one, have appeared on the front of Corn Flakes boxes, and have been voted Entertainer of the Year three times. Their debut album, Brand New Man *(1991) has been certified an impressive quintuple platinum. Ten years after that release, in 2001, Brooks & Dunn released their newest album,* Steers & Stripes, *which debuted at number-one on* Billboard's *Country Album chart and number-four in the top 200 for all-genre sales.*

The duo that knocked Nashville off its feet has accumulated dozens of awards, including two Grammys. They were voted the Country Music Association's Vocal Duo of the Year every year from 1992 to 1999, and the Academy of Country Music's Vocal Duo of the Year every year from 1991 to 1997. In 1995 and 1996, Brooks &

Dunn were named the Academy of Country Music's Entertainer of the Year, and earned the same title with the Country Music Association in 1996. It was the first and only time that this award has gone to a duo.

The first year out, their Neon Circus & Wild West Show tour picked up the International Talent Buyers Association's Country Tour of the Year Award and was the only country tour nominated for Pollstar's Most Creative Tour Package.

With singles such as Ain't Nothing 'Bout You, How Long Gone, My Maria, Hard Workin' Man, *and* Boot Scootin' Boogie, *Kix Brooks and Ronnie Dunn have managed to reach the top and stay there for more than a decade. They obviously spend a great deal of time on the road, but when each steps off his bus, it's family time that is important. And for Kix Brooks, that time includes a special horse that he rode in the* My Maria *video, named Prieto.*

Leon Eric "Kix" Brooks, III was born in Shreveport, Louisiana, and spent a lot of time on his grandfather's dairy farm when he was growing up. At the age of twelve he made his public singing debut at a schoolmates birthday party. He continued to sing in clubs and venues throughout high school, and also began writing songs. By the time they teamed up in February of 1991, Kix and Ronnie each had separate, but viable, solo careers.

Today, Kix and his wife, Barbara, are heavily involved in breeding and showing Quarter Horses, and are seen regularly on the cutting horse circuit. But it wasn't until the early 1990s that horses came into their lives.

"I surprised Barb with a horse one year for Christmas," said Kix. "We went down to my dad's farm in Louisiana for Thanksgiving, I think this was in 1993, and we got there real late at night. I'd planned this all out ahead of time. I had some Longhorn cattle down there so after we got there, I said to her, 'Let's go see the Longhorns.' So I found a flashlight, and led her past this corral where this horse was and the horse came up to the fence. Barb started petting the horse and said, 'Whose horse are you?' And I said, 'Guess.' Well, it was a horse I got for her, it was her first horse and she was thrilled."

The gift of the horse, a beautiful Paint mare named Angel, provided one of Kix and Barbara's closest moments as a couple.

Kix became involved in horses himself and when he went to a remote location in South Texas to film the video for *My Maria*, he fell so much in love with, Prieto, the big, black horse he rode in the video, that he eventually bought him.

"There is just something special about this horse," Kix said of Prieto, whose name means "black" in Spanish. "I still am amazed at everything this horse can do, including rearing on command. He is so well-trained. I just had to bring him home because he provides everything I ever thought a horse should provide—companionship, fun, beauty—it's all there."

Prieto was owned by a man named Happy Strand, who was instrumental in bringing the film industry to Texas. When he died, Kix bought the horse from his wife.

"I was very glad to have gotten him," said Kix. "But I know my manager wishes I'd bought him before we filmed the video. I think he would have come a little cheaper!"

Brooks's Painted Springs Farm is located just outside of Nashville, and is also home to Slim and Howdy, two Longhorns who inhabit their front pasture. In case you are wondering, Slim is the red-blonde one, and Howdy is the black speckled one. In recent years, the farm has become well-known in the Quarter Horse world for their quality cutting horses.

"These are horses that can run, and stop, and turn on a dime," Kix explained. "A good cutting horse can mirror the moves of a cow just perfectly, until the just cow turns away in defeat." He added that riding a cutting horse is an experience like no other, and compared it to a wild carnival ride. "Riding cutting horses is hard a lot harder than it looks," he continued. "They'll flat throw you out of the saddle with their moves."

The Brooks's breed most of their horses to sell, but Kix has found that even though there are a lot of willing buyers, that sometimes the selling part becomes a problem.

"Barb gets too attached to the horses and doesn't want to sell," laughed Kix. "Trying to buy a horse from Barb is more rigorous than getting into Augusta Country Club."

One of the horses that would be difficult to sell, Playboys Lil Peppy, came to Painted Springs Farm as a three-year-old and has a wonderful story. Barbara had showed the mare at a number of major cutting horse events, and not only consistently ended up in the finals, but won a good number of the events. But after one of the competitions, the mare kicked through her stall and injured her hind leg.

"There were some cuts on her leg, but nothing that led us to believe that she couldn't continue her training schedule," said Kix. "She was going along just fine."

But several weeks later, her trainer noticed some hesitation when he asked the mare to back up.

"We took her to the vet and found she had a little fracture to her cannon bone," Kix said. "She had done so well for us and we were concerned about her, but we rested her and she healed up very well and now is back at it."

And so are the Brooks's. In the fall of 2001 Kix and Barbara hosted the first annual Music City Futurity. The event featured nine days of cutting competitions, and Kix and Barbara were heavily involved in everything from planning to execution. More than five hundred participants came from as far away as California, Oregon, New Mexico and Rhode Island. In cutting horse circles, the Saturday night concert, with none other than Brooks & Dunn, was not only a highlight of the event, but of the entire year. After the event Kix and Barbara presented Vanderbilt Children's Hospital and the Ronald McDonald House a check for more than sixty-eight thousand dollars.

That's a lot of money, but Kix probably wouldn't take that for Prieto.

"I have found the perfect horse," he said. "I couldn't ask for more."

www.brooks-dunn.com

Brooks & Dunn Fan Club
P.O. Box 120669
Nashville, TN 37212

*Kix and
Prieto.*

MULTIMEDIA INTERACTIVE

BRINGING YOU
TOMORROW'S TECHNOLOGY TODAY

CHECK OUT WHAT WE CAN DO!

- technologically advanced company
- design, develop and produce high quality, easy-to-use interactive marketing tools
- video production, interactive cd-roms and website development
- authoring of each project from start to finish including scripting, graphic design, filming, music composition and professional radio and television voice narration
- all work done in-house by our staff of professionals
- interactive CD-ROMs in the shape of your logo!

Check out our newest and hottest marketing tool! *Interactive CD-ROM Business Cards. Just slightly bigger than a paper business card, they can hold a complete presentation including narration, video, images, catalogs and more. The possibilities are endless.*

Let MultiMedia-Interactive shape your business future by utilizing the tools of today with the technology of tomorrow.

16508 Township Rd., 287 - Conesville, Ohio - 740-829-2764

www.multimedia-interactive.com
info@multimedia-interactive.com

TheHomeShow

Feel Right At Home

A Lifetime Dream - For the Future

Buying a home is a lifetime dream and a monumental achievement. Manufactured housing is the way of the future, providing a high quality home with a low monthly payment. It's one of the best ways to have the home you want... easily, affordably, and quickly.

Being independent, we buy factory direct from not just one manufacturer, but the best of the top national brands, the best of the best. So you have freedom of choice in your dream home.

Our Promise to You

With a firm commitment to doing it right the first time, we strive to deliver, install and service your new home to the highest standards in the industry. We provide you with our "no excuses guarantee" to assure you of quality service. Our in-house installation and service departments deliver on our promise to provide the best service to each of our customers. Our commitment: No Excuses.

www.thehomeshows.com
5898 Rt. 60 East - Barboursville, WV 25504
(304) 736-3888 or (888) 736-3332

Author Info

Raised in Mound, Minnesota, Lisa Wysocky studied to be a horse trainer at the University of Minnesota. Early success on the national and world championship show circuit soon found Lisa writing articles for horse publications. Her passion for writing led to a second run at college where she studied journalism.

A knee injury cut short Lisa's career as a horse trainer, but she quickly ventured into her second love, that of music. Six years as a correspondent for the *Nashville Banner*, and a solid reputation in the music industry as a writer, pulled Lisa into public relations. Lisa is also active in assisting her clients with their public image and with their interview skills. Recently, Lisa served as general manager of the independent label, Scarlet Moon Records,

In addition to *The Power of Horses*, Lisa has written a mystery, *The Opium Equation*, has edited the second edition of *The Coach John Wooden Pyramid of Success*, and travels nationwide as a public speaker.

Lisa lives in Nashville with her son, and their cat and dog. On the rare occasions that she's not writing or on the phone, she enjoys reading, gardening, hiking, old movies, playing Scrabble, and any activity that includes horses.

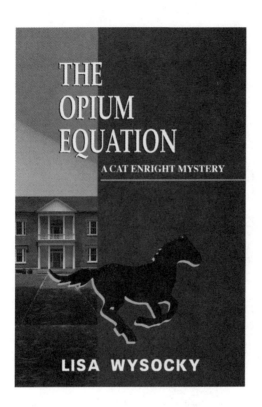

NOVEMBER 2002

The Opium Equation

Introducing the brazenly wacky new sleuth, Cat Enright. A young, single horse trainer based just outside of Nashville, Cat ropes in her eclectic group of friends to help solve the mystery of one neighbor's death and the disappearance of another neighbor's son. In the process, she still has to prepare her horses for the upcoming show season, and gets pulled into the fringes of the country music industry.

Coming Soon:
www.lisawysocky.com and www.theopiumequation.com

To order additional copies of
The Power of Horses
please go to your favorite book retailer,
online bookstore, or www.powerofhorses.com.
Or, mail or fax the order form below.

# OF BOOKS	TITLE	COST PER BOOK	TOTAL
	THE POWER OF HORSES	$17.95	

Please contact us to inquire about discounts on orders of ten or more books. **Coming in November 2002: a mystery, *The Opium Equation*, introducing horse trainer/ sleuth, Cat Enright.**	STATE SALES TAX TN RESIDENTS ONLY	
	SHIPPING: $3.00 PER BOOK (SHIPPING *FREE* FOR ORDERS OF FIVE OR MORE BOOKS)	
	TOTAL DUE	

VISA ❏   MasterCard ❏   Check ❏   Money Order ❏

CARD # [ ][ ][ ][ ] - [ ][ ][ ][ ] - [ ][ ][ ][ ] - [ ][ ][ ][ ]

EXPIRATION DATE _____

NAME ON CARD _____

BILLING ADDRESS _____

  CITY/STATE/ZIP_____

SHIPPING ADDRESS _____

  CITY/STATE/ZIP_____

DAYTIME PHONE NUMBER   (_____)_____

EMAIL ADDRESS _____
❏ CHECK HERE TO ADD YOUR EMAIL ADDRESS TO OUR E-LIST

Please mail to: Fura Books, Inc.
P.O. Box 90751, Nashville, TN 37209
Or fax to: 615.353.8892